TWENTY-FOUR CREATIVE,

INTERACTIVE STORY PROGRAMS

FOR PRESCHOOLERS

ROB REID

AN IMPRINT OF THE AMERICAN LIBRARY ASSOCIATION
CHICAGO   2015

Rob Reid is the very popular author of numerous books on children's programming for ALA Editions. He has also written resources for Upstart Books and is the author of two picture books. In addition, he writes regular columns on programming and children's literature for *LibrarySparks* magazine and has a column in *Book Links* magazine titled "Reid-Aloud Alert." Rob is a senior lecturer at the University of Wisconsin–Eau Claire and conducts workshops across North America on ways to make literature come alive for children. Rob can be contacted through www.rapnrob.com.

© 2015 by the American Library Association

Extensive effort has gone into ensuring the reliability of the information in this book; however, the publisher makes no warranty, express or implied, with respect to the material contained herein.

ISBN: 978-0-8389-1271-3 (paper)

Library of Congress Cataloging-in-Publication Data
Reid, Rob.
  Animal shenanigans : twenty-four creative, interactive story programs for preschoolers / Rob Reid.
    pages cm
  Includes bibliographical references and index.
  ISBN 978-0-8389-1271-3
  1. Children's libraries—Activity programs—United States. 2. Storytelling—United States. 3. Libraries and preschool children—United States. 4. Animals—Juvenile literature—Bibibliography. 5. Picture books for children—United States—Bibliography. I. Title.
  Z718.3.R44 2015
  027.62'50973—dc23
                        2014031541

Cover design by Kimberly Thornton. Cover illustrations © Bistraffic / Shutterstock. Text design and composition in the Dante MT, Myriad Pro, and True North typefaces by Ryan Scheife / Mayfly Design.

♾ This paper meets the requirements of ANSI/NISO Z39.48–1992 (Permanence of Paper).

Printed in the United States of America

19 18 17 16 15   5 4 3 2 1

For Harris

CONTENTS

THE PROGRAMS

ACKNOWLEDGMENTS

Thanks go out to:

My grandsons Parker, Wesley, and Harris for pretending to be animals with their grandpa;

Colleen and Uncle Squaty, multiple Parents' Choice Award winners, for their kind permission to reprint "Five Tall Giraffes" from their recording *Shake It Down, Turn Around* (North Side Music, 2010);

LibrarySparks magazine for making me part of their family for the past decade. The following activities originally appeared in articles I wrote for *LibrarySparks* and are reprinted with their kind permission: "Animal Snores" from the December 2007 issue and "Goldilocks" from the January 2012 issue;

Upstart Books for their kind permission to reprint two activities from books I have written for them: "Dogs and Cats and Guinea Pigs" from *Storytime Slam!* (2006) and "The Raccoon's Hunt" from *Welcome to Storytime* (2012);

My ALA Editions family and the students in my 2014 ALA e-course "Storytime Shenanigans" for helping develop a creative atmosphere of fingerplay creation;

The L.E. Phillips Memorial Public Library (Eau Claire, Wisconsin), the Altoona (Wisconsin) Public Library, and the Indianhead Federated Library System (Wisconsin) for providing a steady stream of picture books;

Little Bloomers Child Care Center, Flynn Elementary, Sam Davey Elementary, and the Trinity Equestrian Center, all of Eau Claire, Wisconsin, for the guinea pigs;

Members of the Animal Kingdom, except for you, Wisconsin mosquitoes.

INTRODUCTION

I was flipping through the shelves of new picture books at my local library when I was struck by the high number of books that featured animals. Granted, animals have always been popular with children and have been a staple in children's books for decades. But I couldn't get over the high percentage of titles featuring both realistic and anthropomorphic critters. One thing led to another, and I was off creating a new series of story program lesson plans featuring our four-legged, no-legged, winged, scaled, and feathered friends.

The preschool lesson plans (they also work well for K–2 grade levels) are in the style of my previous ALA Editions story programming books, such as *Family Storytime, More Family Storytimes, Something Musical Happened at the Library,* and *What's Black and White and Reid All Over?* Each program is approximately thirty minutes in length and is composed of a mix of "newer" picture books (all published between 2010 and 2014) and "in-between" activities. I had a blast creating seventy new "in-between" activities—fingerplays and movement activities, songs and musical activities, chants, creative dramatics, and imagination exercises.

Please feel free to use these and all of the ideas in *Animal Shenanigans* in your own story programs.

And while you're using them, have a howling, barking, clucking, roaring good time!

THE PROGRAMS

LET'S ACT LIKE ANIMALS

STORIES AND ACTIVITIES
ABOUT IMAGINATION

Opening Picture Book

The Purple Kangaroo by Michael Ian Black. Illustrated by Peter Brown.
Simon & Schuster, 2010.

A monkey talks directly to you, the reader, and brags, "I can read minds. It's true. In fact, I can read YOUR mind." The monkey asks you to think of something so spectacular "that nobody has ever thought of it in the entire history of thinking about things." The monkey guesses that you are thinking of a purple kangaroo. Not only that, you are thinking of "a purple kangaroo looking for his best friend, a wild-eyed chinchilla named Señor Ernesto de Pantalones." The monkey goes on to elaborate that you are thinking of the purple kangaroo wearing roller skates, juggling bananas, blowing a bubble-gum bubble out its nose, riding in a blimp, and flying to the moon. The book's punch line is that if you, the reader, weren't thinking of that before, you're thinking of it now.

> **STORYTELLING TIPS:** Read the monkey's voice as a salesperson or huckster—in other words, in a "slick," energetic style.

Picture Book

I'm a Frog! by Mo Willems. Illustrated by the author. Hyperion, 2013.

Piggie pretends that he is a frog and hops around while saying "Ribbit." His friend Gerald is confused and then worried. "What if I become a frog? Hopping all day . . . Eating flies!" Piggie teaches Gerald about "pre-tend," when someone acts like something he or she is not. Gerald responds with "And you can just *do* that?" Gerald refuses to act like a frog, instead preferring to act like a cow.

Movement Activity

"Tiny Little Frogs" by Rob Reid.

Tell everyone to imagine they are frogs. Start with everyone down in a "pre-hopping position," similar to the image of Piggie on the cover of *I'm a Frog!* After the first verse, lead the kids into imagining themselves as other animals.

Tiny little frogs,
Jumping up and down, (*Jump up and down.*)
Making funny sounds, (*Make frog noises—"Ribbit," "Croak," etc.*)
Tiny little frogs.

Tiny little calves,
Leaping up and down, (*Move around on all fours in little bursts.*)
Making funny sounds, (*Moo.*)
Tiny little calves.

Tiny little ducklings,
Waddling all around, (*Waddle with arms tucked in as wings.*)
Making funny sounds, (*Quack.*)
Tiny little ducklings.

Tiny little owls,
Swooping all around, (*Hold arms out as wings and glide around.*)
Making funny sounds, (*Hoot.*)
Tiny little owls.

Tiny little monkeys,
Swinging all around, (*Pretend to swing from overhead branches.*)
Making funny sounds, (*Make monkey noises like "Ooo-ooo."*)
Tiny little monkeys.

Tiny little mice,
Scurrying all around, (*Back on all fours, make little darting movements.*)
Making funny sounds, (*Squeak.*)
Tiny little mice.

Ask the children to use their imaginations and come up with other animals to act out in this rhyme pattern.

Picture Book / Movement Activity

It's a Tiger! by David LaRochelle. Illustrated by Jeremy Tankard. Chronicle, 2012.

- -

A child pretends that he (or she) is in the jungle "where the tall trees grow and the monkeys swing from vine to vine." The child looks closer and realizes that he's not looking at a monkey; it's "a tiger! Run!" He leads us to a cave where we see shadows. One of the shadows turns out to be the tiger! We climb out of the cave and tiptoe past snakes. Unfortunately, one of the snakes turns out to be the tiger's tail. We run once more and swing onto a pile of orange leaves. Yes, the leaves turn out to be a tiger. We get a ride on a boat but notice that the captain has a tail. "A TIGER! Not AGAIN!" We jump overboard and swim to an island. We open a treasure chest and, yes, find the tiger inside. We learn he doesn't want to eat us. He wants us to rub his belly. The boy starts telling the tiger a different story. This one has us back in the jungle watching out for "A CROCODILE!"

Song

"Use, Use, Use Your Mind, Part One" by Rob Reid.

- -

Sing to the tune of the traditional song "Row, Row, Row Your Boat." The melody can be found on the Internet as well as the following children's music recordings: *I Found You* by Caspar Babypants (Aurora Elephant Music, 2013), *Rise and Shine* by Raffi (Troubadour, 1982), and *Wee Sing and Pretend* by Pamela Beall and Susan Nipp (Price Stern Sloan, 2001). As you chant each verse, pause after the phrase "Tell me what you say" and let the kids fill in with the proper animal sound.

Use, use, use your mind,
In a special way,
Imagine that you are a Bee,
Tell me what you say: *"Buzz!"*

Use, use, use your mind,
In a special way,
Imagine that you are a Coyote,
Tell me what you say: *"Howl!"* (or *"Yip! Yip!"*)

Use, use, use your mind,
In a special way,
Imagine that you are a Dolphin,
Tell me what you say: *"Eee! Eee! Eee!"* (or *"Click! Click! Click!"*)

Use, use, use your mind,
In a special way,
Imagine that you are a Donkey,
Tell me what you say: *"Hee-haw!"*

Use, use, use your mind,
In a special way,
Imagine that you are a Llama,
Tell me what you say: "_____!" (*Make a pretend spit noise. Entirely optional, of course, but the kids will laugh.*)

Ask your audience if they can add any other animals and their sounds to the song.

Picture Book

Ernest, the Moose Who Doesn't Fit by Catherine Rayner. Illustrated by the author. Farrar, Straus and Giroux, 2010.

- -

Ernest the moose is RATHER LARGE and does not fit on the pages of the book. "Luckily, Ernest is also a very determined moose. He's not going to give up easily." With the help of a little chipmunk, Ernest shifts, shuffles, and squeezes back and forth on the pages, but we still only see his middle. The chipmunk comes up with a creative idea, and the two grab some masking tape and paper. They finally finish their project. We learn they made a large foldout page at the very end of the book. "Ernest may be a RATHER LARGE moose . . . but now he has a RATHER LARGE book . . . and he fits in perfectly."

STORYTELLING TIPS: As you read about Ernest's efforts to fit on the pages, tighten your voice to show his struggles. When you begin to unfold the final pages, slow down and build up the excitement as we finally see Ernest's entire body for the first time.

Musical Activity

"Use, Use, Use Your Mind, Part Two" by Rob Reid.

- -

Sing to the tune of the traditional song, "Row, Row, Row Your Boat."

Use, use, use your mind,
To a special groove,
Imagine you're an Alligator,
Show me how you move!
(*Make alligator jaws out of arms, open and shut them.*)

Use, use, use your mind,
To a special groove,
Imagine you're a Butterfly,
Show me how you move!
(*Flap arms as you slowly move around the room.*)

Use, use, use your mind,
To a special groove,
Imagine you're a Hummingbird,
Show me how you move!
(*Flap arms very quickly as you dart around the room.*)

Use, use, use your mind,
To a special groove,
Imagine you're a Lobster,
Show me how you move!
(*Click thumbs on both hands as if they were claws.*)

Use, use, use your mind,
To a special groove,
Imagine you're a Turtle,
Show me how you move!
(*Get on all fours, move slowly, stop and pull head into shoulders.*)

Use, use, use your mind,
To a special groove,
Imagine you're a Cheetah,
Show me how you move!
(*Run around the room in a circle as fast as you can!*)

Closing Picture Book / Movement Activity

You Are a Lion! And Other Fun Yoga Poses by Taeeun Yoo. Illustrated by the author. Nancy Paulsen, 2012.

- -

Children gather in a garden and perform a variety of yoga poses. When a child sits on his heels with his hands on his knees and tongue out, he is told to imagine he is a lion. Another child sits with feet together, holding her toes, and flapping her legs. She becomes a butterfly. Other yoga scenarios have the children imagine they are a dog, a snake, a frog, and a cat. The children also stand and reach. "You are a . . . / Mountain / Soaring up high / Solid and mighty / Touching the sky." At the end, the children lie on their backs, relaxing in silence.

STORYTELLING TIPS: Have the children perform the same yoga poses along with the characters in the book. Read slowly and wait several seconds before moving on to the next exercise. At the end of the book, when your own audience is on their backs, quietly whisper, "Storytime is over for today."

5 Fun Backup Picture Books

Hey, Rabbit! by Sergio Ruzzier. Illustrated by the author. Roaring Brook, 2010.

- -

A rabbit opens a suitcase for a dog. The dog, who had wished for a bone, is surprised to find a cake lined with several bones. A toucan looks inside the suitcase and finds an entire jungle. A bear gets a bed in a cave, a cat receives several balls of yarn, a mouse gets a room full of cheese, a crab gets an ocean, and Rabbit gets all of his friends— and a giant turnip.

If All the Animals Came Inside by Eric Pinder. Illustrated by Marc Brown. Little, Brown, 2012.

A young boy imagines having lots of fun if animals came inside his house. "The walls would tremble. The windows would shake. Oh, what a terrible mess we would make!" The boy would go on elephant rides and play hide-and-seek with the monkeys in the living room. The panda bear would raid the refrigerator, and the boy's father might accidentally sit on a porcupine. At night, the animals would climb into the boy's bed and hoot and howl all night. They would force the boy and his sister outside the house where "we'd pack up our tent and go play on the lawn."

Little Mouse by Alison Murray. Illustrated by the author. Hyperion, 2013.

A girl's mother calls her "little mouse." The girl, however, feels as tall as a giraffe and as strong as a bull. She chomps on food like a horse and is as brave and scary as a lion. She says, "I don't really sound like a little mouse . . . Trumpety, trump, trump! Too-whit, too-whit, too-woOOo! Yowly, howly, howl! Squeak! Oops! That was a hiccup!" At the end of the day in bed, the girl is content to be as quiet as a mouse.

Little White Rabbit by Kevin Henkes. Illustrated by the author. Greenwillow, 2011.

As a little white rabbit hops through the grass, he imagines what it would be like to be green. We then see a picture of a green rabbit. As the rabbit hops by the fir trees, he wonders what it would be like to be tall. We see a rabbit as tall as the trees. The little white rabbit also wonders what it would be like to be as immovable as a rock and to flutter like a butterfly. He wondered "about many things, but he didn't wonder who loved him."

A Moose That Says Moo by Jennifer Hamburg. Illustrated by Sue Truesdell. Farrar, Straus and Giroux, 2013.

- -

A girl decides to create a zoo in her backyard. "The first thing I'd have is a moose that said 'moo.'" She goes on to imagine other strange animals to put in her zoo. Examples include literate sharks, an ox that is also a short-order cook, jump-roping skunks, tap-dancing pigs, and "an all-duck jazz band." The girl's imagination leads her to come to the conclusion that it would never work out. "And then I'd vow never to do THAT again, until I considered a juggling hen."

THE ANIMAL BOOK CLUB

STORIES AND ACTIVITIES ABOUT READING

- ★ Opening Picture Book: *Open This Little Book* by Jesse Klausmeier and Suzy Lee
- ★ Chant: "Read a Book! Read a Book!" by Rob Reid
- ★ Picture Book: *We Are in a Book!* by Mo Willems
- ★ Picture Book: *Five Little Monkeys Reading in Bed* by Eileen Christelow
- ★ Fingerplay: "Monkeys Reading in Bed," traditional; adapted by Rob Reid
- ★ Picture Book: *Again!* by Emily Gravett
- ★ Picture Book: *It's a Little Book* by Lane Smith
- ★ Closing Sound Effects Rhyme: "My Monkey Likes to Read to Me" by Rob Reid

Opening Picture Book

Open This Little Book by Jesse Klausmeier. Illustrated by Suzy Lee. Chronicle, 2013.

This picture book is formatted so that there are smaller pages representing smaller books inside the regular book. We are instructed to open a red book. The book is about a ladybug that opens a green book. Turn the page and we find a frog that opens an orange book. This pattern continues with a rabbit opening a yellow book, a bear opening a very small blue book, and a giant who can't open her rainbow book because "her hands are way too big!" The animals from the other books help her out, and we wind up closing the blue book, the yellow book, the orange book, the green book, and the red book. At the end, we are encouraged to "open another!"

> **STORYTELLING TIPS:** Read through the book once and then use it for a prop for the accompanying chant.

Chant

"Read a Book! Read a Book!" by Rob Reid.

This chant was inspired by Klausmeier's picture book. Show the different colored books within her picture book and teach the kids the chant.

> "Read a Book, Read a Book. It's Lots of Fun!
> Read a Book, Read a Book. It's Lots of Fun!"

Show the red book to your audience and have them shout the chant.

> "READ A BOOK!! READ A BOOK!! IT'S LOTS OF FUN!!
> READ A BOOK!! READ A BOOK!! IT'S LOTS OF FUN!!"

Show them the green book and have them recite the chant slightly less noisily.

"Read a Book! Read a Book! It's Lots of Fun!
Read a Book! Read a Book! It's Lots of Fun!"

Show them the orange book and have them recite the chant slightly more quietly.

"Read a Book. Read a Book. It's Lots of Fun.
Read a Book. Read a Book. It's Lots of Fun."

Show them the yellow book and have them recite the chant more quietly but louder than a whisper.

"Read a Book. Read a Book. It's Lots of Fun.
Read a Book. Read a Book. It's Lots of Fun."

Show them the blue book and have them whisper the chant.

"Read a Book. Read a Book. It's Lots of Fun.
Read a Book. Read a Book. It's Lots of Fun."

Show them the rainbow book and have them silently mouth the words.

"Read a Book. Read a Book. It's Lots of Fun.
Read a Book. Read a Book. It's Lots of Fun."

Start reversing the process. Show them the blue book being closed in the regular book and whisper the chant.

"Read a Book. Read a Book. It's Lots of Fun.
Read a Book. Read a Book. It's Lots of Fun."

Show them the yellow book again and have them chant a little louder.

"Read a Book. Read a Book. It's Lots of Fun.
Read a Book. Read a Book. It's Lots of Fun."

Show them the orange book again and have them chant a little louder.

"Read a Book. Read a Book. It's Lots of Fun.
Read a Book. Read a Book. It's Lots of Fun."

Show them the green book again and have them chant a little louder.

"Read a Book! Read a Book! It's Lots of Fun!
Read a Book! Read a Book! It's Lots of Fun!"

Show them the red book again and have them yell the chant.

"READ A BOOK!! READ A BOOK!! IT'S LOTS OF FUN!!
READ A BOOK!! READ A BOOK!! IT'S LOTS OF FUN!!"

Have everyone clap and get ready for the next book.

Picture Book

We Are in a Book! by Mo Willems. Illustrated by the author. Hyperion, 2010.

- -

Gerald the elephant realizes that someone is looking at him and his best friend, Piggie. Gerald is told that a *reader* is looking at them.

STORYTELLING TIPS: When Gerald and Piggie laugh hysterically, ask the kids in the audience to laugh, too. This goes on for seven pages. At the end of the book, the reader has to make the decision to read the entire book again or not. Let your kids make that same choice.

Not only that, the reader is *reading* about them. Gerald learns for the first time that they are in a book. Piggie has fun making the reader say "Banana." Gerald cracks up but then becomes panicked when he learns that the book will end soon. The two send out this plea to the reader: "Will you please read us again?"

Picture Book

Five Little Monkeys Reading in Bed by Eileen Christelow. Illustrated by the author. Clarion, 2011.

- -

The five monkey siblings from Christelow's popular series love to read, even after Mama tells them to turn out the lights. They start crying because their book is sad. When the book ends on a positive note, they cheer. Mama rushes in and commands them to turn out the light. "No more reading in bed!" The naughty monkeys pull out a scary book and make more noise. Mama scolds them once more. It doesn't do any good because the siblings share a funny book that makes them laugh out loud. Mama has had enough. The little monkeys start to go to sleep when they hear a different noise. It's Mama who is reading in bed.

STORYTELLING TIPS: Those who know the fingerplay rhyme "Five Little Monkeys Jumping on the Bed" can follow the same rhythmic cadence of this text. Have fun sounding sad, then scared, and finally overjoyed with the little monkeys' lines. Mama's scolding lines are also fun to read aloud. "I've had it! That's it!" Let your face duplicate Mama's angry, weary appearance and then her tired smile at the end.

Fingerplay

"Monkeys Reading in Bed," traditional; adapted by Rob Reid.

- -

One little monkey was reading in her bed, (*Hold up one finger.*)
When she was done this is what she said,
"I read a book that was very sad, (*Make a sad face.*)
But it ended well and now I'm glad!" (*Smile and nod.*)

Two little monkeys were reading in bed, (*Hold up two fingers.*)
When they were done this is what they said,
"We read a book that gave us a fright, (*Make a frightened face.*)
It was fun but we'll be up all night!" (*Smile nervously and look around.*)

Three little monkeys were reading in bed, (*Hold up three fingers.*)
When they were done this is what they said,
"We read a book that was lots of fun, (*Smile.*)
It made us laugh and now we're done!" (*Nod.*)

Picture Book

Again! by Emily Gravett. Illustrated by the author. Simon & Schuster, 2013.

- -

A mother dragon reads a bedtime story to her young dragon. That story is about a red dragon that goes on the prowl and grabs princesses. The bedtime book ends with the lines "At the end of the day he shouts out this refrain: 'TOMORROW I'LL DO IT ALL OVER AGAIN!'" The young dragon holds up the bedtime book and says, "Again?" The mother dragon reads it again with minor alterations. The baby demands that the mother dragon read the book again. She reads a brief synopsis version of the story of the red dragon. The baby once more makes demands to have the book read again. The mother dragon falls asleep during the fourth reading. The baby dragon lets loose with a fire exhalation and we find an actual hole in the final pages and back cover of the book we are holding.

Picture Book

It's a Little Book by Lane Smith. Illustrated by the author.
Roaring Brook, 2011.

This board book version of Lane Smith's picture book *It's a Book* depicts that book's characters—the jackass and the monkey—as toddlers clad in diapers. The jackass (the characters are not named in this version) asks about the monkey's book. "What is that? Is it for chewing?" The monkey says "No" to this and all of the other questions that the jackass has about the book. He wants to know if the book is for wearing, e-mailing, quacking, flying, riding, building, calling, or sleeping. The monkey finally tells him, "It's for reading. It's a book, silly."

Closing Sound Effects Rhyme

"My Monkey Likes to Read to Me" by Rob Reid.

- -

My monkey likes to read to me,
She's really very good.
She has me sit and starts to read
Like a monkey should.
She goes: "Ooh-Ooh-Ooh . . ." (*Hold up a book as if you were reading it out loud and make monkey noises. Use intonations like you would if you were really reading the book. Ask the children to join in with the sound effects.*)

My donkey likes to read to me,
He's really very good.
He has me sit and starts to read
Like a donkey should.
He goes: "Hee-haw, hee-haw, hee-haw . . ." (*Hold up a book as if you were reading it out loud and bray like a donkey along with the children.*)

Ask the kids for suggestions of other animals to use for new verses.

5 Fun Backup Picture Books

Calvin Can't Fly: The Story of a Bookworm Birdie by Jennifer Berne. Illustrated by Keith Bendis. Sterling, 2010.

- -

Calvin the starling comes from a big family. He has "three brothers, four sisters, and sixty-seven thousand four hundred and thirty-two cousins." Calvin is different from his relatives because he likes to read books. While the other birds attend flying school, Calvin is in the library. He's sad when the other birds migrate. The other starlings decide to give Calvin a ride. He becomes very helpful in solving disasters on the trip because of the knowledge he gained from reading books.

Dog Loves Books by Louise Yates. Illustrated by the author. Knopf, 2010.

Dog loves everything about books and opens his own bookstore. No one comes to the grand opening. Then a lady comes into the store and orders tea. "'I'm sorry,' said Dog, 'but this is a bookstore. I only sell books.'" The lady leaves. Dog waits and perks up when a man enters the store. Unfortunately, the man only wants directions. Dog begins to read and forgets he's alone.

I'm Not Reading! by Jonathan Allen. Illustrated by the author. Boxer Books, 2013.

Baby Owl plans to read to Owly, his stuffed toy. Tiny Chick walks by and wants to listen to the story. Baby Owl agrees but only if Tiny Chick sits quietly. Tiny Chick's four siblings come along and they, too, want to listen. Next come Tiny Chick's seven cousins, and they pile on Baby Owl's lap. More and more chicks arrive, and they all squash Baby Owl flat. Baby Owl's dad comes to the rescue. The chicks learn to be good listeners.

Warning: Do Not Open This Book! by Adam Lehrhaupt. Illustrated by Matthew Forsythe. Simon & Schuster, 2013.

The narrator warns you to put this book back or you might let the monkeys out. The reader is scolded because the page was turned. "Didn't you see the warning? Stay on this page. You are safe here." When the next page gets turned, several monkeys appear. Turning more pages produces toucans and an alligator. The narrator asks you to follow a plan to catch all of the animals in the book. It involves a banana . . . .

The Wonderful Book by Leonid Gore. Illustrated by the author.
Scholastic, 2010.

- -

A rabbit finds a book in the woods and sees it as a potential "cozy little house." A bear scares the rabbit away and places the book on its head as a hat. When the bear gets distracted by berries, mice use the book for a table and set pieces of cheese on it. They leave, and a fox uses it as a bed. The next day, a worm is about to take a bite out of the book when a human boy grabs the book and starts reading it. It's a story about a rabbit, a bear, mice, a fox, a worm, "and a curious little boy."

THE ANIMAL TALENT SHOW

STORIES AND ACTIVITIES
ABOUT SINGING, DANCING, AND ART

Opening Picture Book

Z Is for Moose by Kelly Bingham. Illustrated by Paul O. Zelinsky.
Greenwillow, 2012.

Different animals and objects line up backstage for a presentation of the alphabet. First, a large anthropomorphic apple appears onstage to represent the letter *A*. Next, a ball represents the letter *B*. A cat shows up for the letter *C*. A moose interrupts the duck that has started to appear on the stage to represent the letter *D*. The zebra in charge of the pageant informs Moose that he's on the wrong page. Moose continues to appear onstage at inappropriate moments. Finally, it's time for the letter *M*. However, when Zebra substitutes a mouse to accompany that letter, Moose goes berserk. Zebra comes up with a good solution for all.

STORYTELLING TIPS: The book is set up with both normal narration and word balloons. Have fun with the dialogue that appears in those word balloons. At one point Moose is stunned and exclaims, "WHAT? WAIT! NO! That was supposed to be me! MOOSE! With an M!" Another time, Moose says "Sniffle" and "Sob" and "Boo hoo." Milk these lines for all they are worth.

Picture Book

Sparky! by Jenny Offill. Illustrated by Chris Appelhans.
Schwartz & Wade, 2014.

A girl gets a pet sloth and names it Sparky. "My sloth arrived by Express Mail." The girl takes Sparky outside to a tree where it promptly falls asleep on a branch. The girl attempts to engage Sparky. She plays King of the Mountain and Hide-and-Seek. Sparky simply sits as the girl shouts, "I won." In contrast, Sparky is very, very good at the game of Statue. When neighbor Mary Potts comes over, Sparky's owner informs Mary that her pet knows a lot of tricks. She advertises "TRAINED SLOTH EXTRAVAGANZA. Countless Tricks to Mystify You—Just 7 days away!" The girl dresses up as the ringmaster, but Sparky fails to perform. The story ends with the girl playing tag with Sparky. "I reached over and tagged him on his claw. 'You're it, Sparky,' I said. And for a long, long time, he was."

STORYTELLING TIPS: Be sure to read the certificates hanging on Mary Potts's wall: "Excellence in Permission-Slip Compliance," "Best Fire Drill Liner-Upper," and "Most Likely to Chew Close-Mouthed in Lunchroom."

Movement Activity

"The Slow Motion Talent Show" by Rob Reid.

- -

Have the children stand. Remind them that Sparky's owner tried to get him to play dead, roll over, and speak. Perhaps he would have done better with other kinds of tricks. Tell the kids to show how Sparky would do some of those tricks, only remember, he's a sloth and moves very, very, very slowly. Shout out "Juggle!" and lead everyone in miming juggling balls in the air in slow motion. Next, shout out "Dance!" Have everyone slowly dance in the style of their choice (most of them will just wiggle—I speak from experience). Next, shout out "Play the trombone!" and mime moving the slide back and forth slowly. Next, shout "Play the drums!" and continue miming the proper motions slowly. Finally, announce that everyone is going to perform magic and pull a rabbit out of a hat. Mime this action even slower than the previous talents. The kids will find it funny as the imaginary rabbit slowly emerges. In fact, the giggles will be constant throughout this whole activity.

Picture Book

Brontorina **by James Howe. Illustrated by Randy Cecil. Candlewick, 2010.**

- -

A very large dinosaur shows up at Madame Lucille's Dance Academy for Girls and Boys. With some reluctance, Madame Lucille enrolls

Brontorina Apatosaurus. The children in the academy welcome Brontorina. They know that on the outside she is a dinosaur, but in her heart, she is a ballerina. When Brontorina's large size becomes an issue, Madame Lucille exclaims, "The problem is not that you are too big. The problem is that my studio is too small." The dancers move outside to a farm and erect a sign that reads "Madame Lucille's Outdoor Dance Academy for Girls and Boys and Dinosaurs (and Cows)."

STORYTELLING TIPS: Be sure to read the occasional tiny word balloons. Most of these lines are spoken by the children in the academy. Read them with a slightly higher pitched voice.

Musical Activity

"The Ants Go Dancing," traditional; adapted by Rob Reid.

- -

Sing to the tune of the traditional song "The Ants Go Marching." The melody can be found on the Internet as well as the following children's music recordings: *Bouncy Blue* by Mr. Eric and Mr. Michael (Learning Groove, 2010) and *Wee Sing Silly Songs* by Pamela Beall and Susan Nipp (Price Stern Sloan, 1982). Have the children stand and inform them that not only can dinosaurs dance, but teeny-tiny ants can dance as well. As you sing, allow the children to dance around the room in any style they like. Have the children make teeny-tiny dance motions when dancing as ants. Ask them, "How would a teeny-tiny ant dance?" Make sure everyone twirls during the fourth line.

> The ants go dancing one by one, hurrah, hurrah,
> The ants go dancing one by one, hurrah, hurrah,
> The ants go dancing one by one,
> They twirl and spin and have lots of fun,
> As they all go dancing round and round and round.

Next, ask the children how penguins might dance and demonstrate a penguin-style waddle with arms to your sides.

The penguins go dancing one by one, hurrah, hurrah,
The penguins go dancing one by one, hurrah, hurrah,
The penguins go dancing one by one,
They twirl and spin and have lots of fun,
As they all go dancing round and round and round.

Next, dance as a moose might dance. Place hands with fingers splayed on head to represent antlers.

The moose go dancing one by one, hurrah, hurrah,
The moose go dancing one by one, hurrah, hurrah,
The moose go dancing one by one,
They twirl and spin and have lots of fun,
As they all go dancing round and round and round.

Finally, dance as a large dinosaur like Brontorina might dance, with overly large movements. Sing with a deep voice.

The dinosaurs go dancing one by one, hurrah, hurrah,
The dinosaurs go dancing one by one, hurrah, hurrah,
The dinosaurs go dancing one by one,
They twirl and spin and have lots of fun,
As they all go dancing round and round and round.

Picture Book / Movement Activity

Flora and the Flamingo by Molly Idle. Chronicle, 2013.

- -

A girl wearing a pink swimsuit, bathing cap, and flippers approaches a flamingo and imitates the bird's posture and movements in this wordless flap-book. At one point, the flamingo squawks at the girl. She goes tumbling and looks sad. The flamingo apparently feels bad and reaches out to the girl. They put on a dancing performance and take a bow at the end.

Closing Movement Activity

"The Talent Show ABC" by Rob Reid.

Inform the children that they will pretend to be different animals showing a variety of skills for a talent show. Because a lot of the movements might be hard for young children to fully understand, perform a motion and let them follow your lead.

1. An Anteater Acting . . . (*Strike noble pose and say, "To be or not to be."*)
2. A Bear twirling a Baton . . . (*Mime twirling a baton.*)
3. A Camel doing the Can-Can . . . (*Kick one leg up and then the other.*)
4. A Duck Disco dancing . . . (*Strike a pose and point one finger straight up and one down.*)
5. An Elephant playing an Electric guitar . . . (*Mime playing a guitar.*)
6. A Frog swinging on the Flying trapeze . . . (*Move back and forth miming holding on to a trapeze bar overhead.*)
7. A Gorilla striking a Gong . . . (*Take a big swing with hand as if striking a gong.*)
8. A Hippopotamus Hula dancing. . . (*Mime hula dancing with two hands moving downward in one direction and then the other.*)
9. An Iguana Ice-skating . . . (*Place hands behind back and mime skating.*)
10. A Jellyfish Juggling . . . (*Mime juggling balls in the air.*)
11. A Kangaroo telling Knock-Knock jokes . . . (*Tell your favorite "knock-knock" joke.*)

12. A Llama performing Lasso tricks . . . (*Mime twirling a lasso overhead.*)
13. A Moose Miming . . . (*Hold up two palms flat in front of you as if encountering a wall.*)
14. A Newt doing Needlework . . . (*Mime sewing.*)
15. An Owl singing Opera . . . (*Lift head, stretch out arms, and sing a loud note.*)
16. A Porcupine presenting a Puppet show . . . (*Hold up both hands as if you have a puppet on each one.*)
17. A Quail Quizzing the audience . . . (*Ask them, "What's the president's name?"*)
18. A Rhino telling a Riddle . . . (*Tell your favorite kids' riddle.*)
19. A Skunk Skipping . . . (*Skip.*)
20. A Tiger walking on a Tightrope . . . (*Mime walking on a rope one foot in front of the other with outstretched arms trying to maintain balance.*)
21. An Umbrellabird riding a Unicyle . . . (*Hold arms out to each side and move back and forth.*)
22. A Vulture playing the Violin . . . (*Mime playing a violin.*)
23. A Walrus Whistling . . . (*Whistle a simple tune.*)
24. An X-Ray Tetra playing the Xylophone . . . (*Mime playing a xylophone.*)
25. A Yak doing Yo-Yo tricks . . . (*Mime playing with a yo-yo.*)
26. A Zebra saying "Zee End!" (*All take a bow.*)

5 Fun Backup Picture Books

Cock-a-Doodle Dance! **by Christine Tricarico. Illustrated by Rich Deas. Feiwel & Friends, 2012.**

- -

A rooster is weary from the farm routine. He exclaims, "Cock-a-Doo-dle-DULL!" One day, the rooster catches the jitterbug and instructs the other animals to "Cock-a-Doodle DANCE!" The animals love to dance. They perform the "tango wango," the "cha-cha," and the "rumba." The cows even start clogging. The animals are exhausted from dancing two days straight. They all agree to do their chores during the day and dance at night. Unfortunately, the farmer and his wife catch the "jumpin' jitterbug" and leave their "housework incomplete."

Cookie the Walker by Chris Monroe. Illustrated by the author.
Carolrhoda, 2013.

Cookie the dog becomes famous when she begins to walk upright on two legs. She catches the attention of a dog trainer and appears on a television show. Cookie walks on a "flaming board across a kiddie pool filled with some confused, recently borrowed-from-the-lake snapping turtles." She then performs on Cirque De La Toot and eventually gets her own television show. When Cookie becomes homesick, her friend Kevin suggests that she "stand down." When she does so, Cookie is fired from her show. However, she's happier being a normal dog. That doesn't mean she can't stand up and walk around every once in a while to help herself to some "unattended bacon."

Hedgehog's Magic Tricks by Ruth Paul. Illustrated by the author.
Candlewick, 2012.

Hedgehog performs a magic show for an audience made up of young animals. His first trick is to make Mouse disappear. "'Abracadabra!' says Hedgehog. 'Am I still here?' asks Mouse." When that trick doesn't work, Hedgehog tries it again with Rabbit and pulls Rabbit out of the hat by his ears. "'Ouch!' says Rabbit." The other animals feel sorry for Hedgehog and bring him a cake. They all laugh when they realize that the cake is disappearing.

Let's Dance, Grandma! by Nigel McMullen. Illustrated by the author.
HarperCollins, 2014.

A young wolf named Lucy loves to dance. She asks her grandma to join her. Grandma prefers to play ball, ride around like a horse, and play dress-up, cards, and hide-and-seek. Lucy decides that grandmas don't dance and asks to cuddle. Grandma picks up Lucy and hums a lullaby. They sway back and forth "until it seemed to Lucy that the whole world was dancing." Grandma assures Lucy that she only dances with special people.

Teach Your Buffalo to Play Drums by Audrey Vernick. Illustrated by Daniel Jennewein. Balzer & Bray, 2011.

- -

Your buffalo is probably very talented and "born to play drums. You have to teach him how." Set up his drum kit for him, hand him the drumsticks, and provide a soundproof room for him to practice. The illustrations reveal that a practice room was dug deep beneath the house, like a bomb shelter. We are told that if one cannot build a practice room, give the neighbors earmuffs. Finally, your buffalo should join a band where they will all create a magic sound. "If the magic's not happening, those earmuffs might come in handy." The final illustration shows that the buffalo might be better suited to doing a juggling act.

ANIMAL COUNTDOWN

STORIES AND ACTIVITIES ABOUT NUMBERS

Opening Picture Book

Count the Monkeys by Mac Barnett. Illustrated by Kevin Cornell.
Hyperion, 2013.

The narrator invites the reader to count the monkeys. However, when we turn the page, we don't see any monkeys because "1 King Cobra has scared off all the monkeys." The cobra leaves when two mongooses (the narrator asks, "Or is it mongeese?") chase the snake away. Three crocodiles scare the mongooses, four grizzly bears take over for the crocodiles, five swarms of bees drive off the bears, six "sweet old beekeepers" shoo away the bees, seven wolves send the ladies packing ("Wolves and grandmothers never get along!"), eight lumberjacks take care of the wolves, and then invite a ninth lumberjack. The narrator asks if readers have any idea how to get rid of the lumberjacks, and "10 Polka-Dotted Rhinoceroses with Bagpipes and Bad Breath" clear them out. The book is over, and the narrator laments, "Now we'll never get to count the monkeys."

STORYTELLING TIPS: Just follow the narrator's playful voice and pause to let the kids perform the actions and sound effects suggested by the narrator. These include moving hands in a zigzag pattern to confuse the crocodiles, making loud roars to scare the bears, humming happy tunes to keep the bees happy, thanking the beekeepers, giving the lumberjacks high fives, and more. When you read the last line about not getting to count the monkeys, hold up the back endpapers so they face the audience out of sight from your view. The kids will spot dozens of monkeys and holler. Do a double take when you get a good look at the endpapers.

Picture Book

Hide & Seek by Il Sung Na. Illustrated by the author. Knopf, 2012.

Chameleon suggests that all of the animals play a game of hide-and-seek. "'I'll count!' offers Elephant. '1 . . . ' The animals run and hide."

The animals ponder where to hide as Elephant continues to count. Finally, Elephant finishes. "'10!' he cries. 'Ready or not, here I come!'" One by one, he finds all of the animals except Chameleon. Chameleon has camouflaged himself on a branch and cries out, "Found you!" at the end.

> **STORYTELLING TIPS:** Sharp-eyed readers can spot Chameleon on the various double-page spreads as Elephant counts. Hold up each picture for a long time before turning the pages to see if the audience members can spot Chameleon. He reappears in the background after the other animals have been found.

Fingerplay

"Hide and Seek" by Rob Reid.

One, two, three, four, (*Hold up four fingers on your left hand, one at a time.*)

Hide and seek! (*Spread the four fingers of the left hand and place over your left eye horizontally, like half of a mask.*)

Five, six, seven, eight, (*Hold up four fingers on right hand, one at a time.*)

Do not peek! (*Spread the fingers of the right hand and place over your right eye horizontally. Both hands form a mask.*)

Nine, ten, ready or not, (*Drop hands from eyes and hold up two thumbs, one at a time.*)

Here I come!

I see you, there you are, (*Point at audience.*)

Let's start again with one! (*Hold up one finger. Repeat the entire fingerplay, slightly faster.*)

Picture Book

999 Frogs Wake Up by Ken Kimura. Illustrated by Yasunari Murakami. NorthSouth, 2013.

It is spring and time for the animals to wake up. Mother Frog counts her 999 "froglets" but finds only 998. She hears snoring and finds Big Brother asleep. When he wakes up, Mother Frog and her 999 frogs hear more snoring. They wake up an old turtle. Once again, they hear snoring and, in turn, wake up a lizard, several ladybugs, and a snake. The snake asks if it is mealtime, and Mother Frog convinces him to go back to sleep. The turtle carries the sleeping snake deep into the woods. Mother Frog begins counting her children, but still comes up with 998. Big Brother has once again fallen asleep.

STORYTELLING TIPS: When you read the snoring lines— "Zzz…zzz…zzz!"—ask the children to join you. During the pattern of waking up the various animals, ask the children to yell, "Wake up, sleepyhead!" even though the text doesn't follow those exact words each time.

Imagination Exercise

"Animal Letters One through Nine" by Rob Reid.

Take the first letters of the numerals one through nine and ask the children in your audience to name an animal that begins with that letter. For very young children, have pictures of several animals that fit this exercise hung on the walls and don't be afraid to point to some of the correct answers for them. For older children, let them think for a while without visual clues. When you read the first line of each two-line ditty, pause before you say the correct letter and let the children supply an answer.

One starts with the letter . . . *O!*

Who can name a bird or animal that also starts with *O*? (*Possible answers: Octopus, Orangutan, Ostrich, Otter, Owl, Ox.*)

Two and *Three* start with the letter . . . *T*!

Who can name a bird or animal that also starts with *T*? (*Possible answers: Termite, Tiger, Turkey, Turtle.*)

Four and *Five* start with the letter . . . *F*!

Who can name a bird or animal that also starts with *F*? (*Possible answers: Fish, Flamingo, Fly, Fox, Frog.*)

Six and *Seven* start with the letter . . . *S*!

Who can name a bird or animal that also starts with *S*? (*Possible answers: Scorpion, Seal, Shark, Sheep, Skunk, Snail, Snake, Spider, Squid, Squirrel.*)

Eight starts with the letter . . . *E*!

Who can name a bird or animal that also starts with *E*? (*Possible answers: Eagle, Eel, Egret, Elephant, Elk, Emu.*)

Nine starts with the letter . . . *N*!

Who can name a bird or animal that also starts with *N*? (*Possible answers: Newfoundland, Newt, Nighthawk, Nightingale, Nuthatch.*)

Picture Book

Baby Bear Counts One by Ashley Wolff. Illustrated by the author. Beach Lane, 2013.

- -

Baby Bear hears a "Thockthockthockthockthock" in the woods and counts one woodpecker. There is a "plunk . . . plunk" noise as he is hit in the head by acorns dropped by two squirrels. Baby Bear hears a

STORYTELLING TIPS: Each animal has its own noise. Read those sound effect lines and then pause. Let the kids in the audience repeat the sounds before you move on. Even the snowflakes have their own noise: "Ting!"

"Whap! Whap! Whap!" and thinks someone is clapping for him. His mother explains that three beavers are gathering twigs. Baby Bear goes on to count four and then five deer crunching corn in the fields, six turkeys gobbling, seven bees buzzing, eight frogs going "Ker-plip! Ker-plop!," nine geese honking, and ten snowflakes falling from the sky. Soon, there are too many snowflakes to count, and Baby Bear and his mother curl up in their den.

Closing Movement Activity / Imagination Exercise

"A Little Bear Cub Climbed Up a Tall Tree" by Rob Reid.
- -
Everyone stands.

A little bear cub climbed up a tall tree, (*Mime climbing.*)
The cub looked around, (*Swivel head.*)
Tell me what did she see?
She saw one wolf. (*Hold up one finger, throw head back, and howl.*)

A little lion cub climbed up a tall tree, (*Mime climbing.*)
The cub looked around, (*Swivel head.*)
Tell me what did he see?
He saw two elephants. (*Hold up two fingers and then hold arm in front of nose and make a trumpeting noise.*)

A little koala cub climbed up a tall tree, (*Mime climbing.*)
The cub looked around, (*Swivel head.*)
Tell me what did she see?
She saw three kangaroos. (*Hold up three fingers and hop around, saying, "Boing, boing, boing."*)

A little parrot chick flew up a tall tree, (*Mime flying.*)
The chick looked around, (*Swivel head.*)
Tell me what did she see?

She saw four snakes. (*Hold up four fingers and then put both palms together and move them back and forth. Make a hissing noise.*)

A little whale calf swam down into the sea, (*Mime diving.*)
The calf looked around, (*Swivel head.*)
Tell me what did he see?
He saw five sharks. (*Hold up five fingers and then cross arms with elbows on top of each other. Move them up and down.*)

5 Fun Backup Picture Books

10 Hungry Rabbits: Counting and Color Concepts by Anita Lobel.
Illustrated by the author. Knopf, 2012.

Mama needs help getting ingredients from the garden for her soup. Her ten hungry children hop off and find one purple cabbage, two white onions, three yellow peppers, four red tomatoes, five pink potatoes, six orange carrots, seven brown mushrooms, eight blueberries, nine green peas, and ten black peppercorns. In no time, the "happy rabbits were hungry no more."

The House of 12 Bunnies by Caroline Stills and Sarcia Stills-Blott.
Illustrated by Judith Rossell. Holiday House, 2012.

Sophie has lost something. She goes from room to room in search of this elusive item. Each room contains several objects. "In the kitchen, there are 5 cups, 4 plates, 2 bowls, and a mug without a handle." After searching inside and out, Sophie finds her book under her pillow in the bedroom. "In a warm, cozy bed, there are 12 snuggly bunnies and 1 bedtime story."

Let's Count Goats! by Mem Fox. Illustrated by Jan Thomas. Beach Lane, 2010.

There are a variety of goats to count. There is a mountain goat "frisking in the sun" and a city goat that goes "for a run." There are also seaside goats, drinking goats, eating goats, little goats, airport goats, pilot goats, show-off goats, rowdy goats, crossing goats, sand-pit goats, trumpet goats, and more.

One Pup's Up by Marsha Wilson Chall. Illustrated by Henry Cole. Margaret K. McElderry, 2010.

One by one, ten puppies start playing "in a fuzzy puppy jumble." After they come back inside, they all line up "in the Line-'em-up Café" (a row of bowls). The countdown goes back from ten to one as first "10 pups nudge, 9 puppies nibble, 8 puppies beg for more yummy puppy kibble," down to the "last pup sags." All ten puppies are asleep as they were in the beginning of the book—"until . . . 1 pup's up" and the fun begins all over again.

Ten Things I Love about You by Daniel Kirk. Illustrated by the author. Nancy Paulsen, 2013.

Rabbit makes a list of ten things he loves about Pig. The first (and only) item on the list is "I love Pig because he is very pink." Rabbit informs Pig that he will continue to add to the list, but he needs Pig's help. Pig is too busy to help but that only gives Rabbit more reasons to add to his list. "I love Pig because he knows how to keep busy." Rabbit eventually learns that Pig has been working on a similar list about him. The tenth reason becomes "I love Pig because he's my friend."

IT'S NOT EASY BEING GREEN (OR RED OR BLUE OR YELLOW)

STORIES AND ACTIVITIES ABOUT COLORS

Opening Picture Book

Pink Me Up **by Charise Mericle Harper. Illustrated by the author. Knopf, 2010.**

A young girl rabbit is excited for the "3rd Annual Pink Girls Pink-Nic." Unfortunately, her mother has pink spots all over. "Oh no! Mama is sick. She cannot go to our pink-nic. Today is the worst day EVER!" Daddy volunteers to take the girl, but she points out "something very important: Daddy! You're a boy!" The party is for girls, not boys. Daddy wears his pink tie. It's not pink enough, so they draw pink polka dots on his shirt, tape pink stripes to his pants, wrap pink paper on his shoes, and add pink stickers to his jacket. "Now Daddy is perfectly PINK. But not as pink as me!" At the pink-nic, Daddy is a hit. The mothers of the other girls tell him that he's "pink-tastic" and "pink-abulous." Afterward, the other girls race home to "pink up" their daddies. The book ends with the girl thinking, "we'll all live pinkishly ever after."

> **STORYTELLING TIPS:** Wear something pink as you read this story.

Picture Book

Purple Little Bird **by Greg Foley. Illustrated by the author. Balzer & Bray, 2011.**

Purple Little Bird "lived in a purple little house with a purple little fence and a very purple garden." However, something is not quite right with his house. He leaves to look for "a truly perfect place." He finds Brown Bear living in a brown cave. Purple Little Bird declares that it's too dark. He finds Gray Goat up a gray steep cliff. The bird learns that it's too windy up there. Purple Little Bird finds Yellow

> **STORYTELLING TIPS:** In addition to wearing something pink, wear something purple.

Camel in the yellow desert but finds it to be too dusty. Blue Frog in his blue pond is next—"It's too damp!" Three Pink Possums hanging from their pink tree lead Purple Little Bird to a place they know about: Purple Little Bird's very own house! Purple Little Bird realizes that his house has too much purple and adds the different colors he observed on his trip.

Song

"Mary Wore Her Red Dress (Mary Was a Bird)," traditional; adapted by Rob Reid.

- -

Sing the tune or simply chant the words. The melody to this traditional song can be found on the Internet and on the recording *Everything Grows* by Raffi (Troubadour, 1987). Tell the children in your audience that Purple Little Bird wasn't the only colorful bird out there.

Mary wore her red dress, red dress, red dress,
Mary wore her red dress all day long.
Mary was a red bird, red bird, red bird,
Mary was a red bird all day long. (*Hold up a picture of a cardinal.*)

Noah wore his blue pants, blue pants, blue pants,
Noah wore his blue pants all day long.
Noah was a blue bird, blue bird, blue bird,
Noah was a blue bird all day long. (*Hold up a picture of a bluebird.*)

Owen wore his green shirt, green shirt, green shirt,
Owen wore his green shirt all day long.
Owen was a green bird, green bird, green bird,
Owen was a green bird all day long. (*Hold up a picture of a parrot.*)

Lilly wore her yellow hat, yellow hat, yellow hat,
Lilly wore her yellow hat all day long.

Lilly was a yellow bird, yellow bird, yellow bird,
Lilly was a yellow bird all day long. (*Hold up a picture of a goldfinch.*)

Chloe wore her pink coat, pink coat, pink coat,
Chloe wore her pink coat all day long.
Chloe was a pink bird, pink bird, pink bird,
Chloe was a pink bird all day long. (*Hold up a picture of a flamingo.*)

Picture Book

Moo, Moo, Brown Cow, Have You Any Milk? **by Phillis Gershator.**
Illustrated by Giselle Potter. Random House, 2011.

The story opens with a boy singing the traditional nursery rhyme "Baa, Baa, Black Sheep." The black sheep says that the wool can be turned into a blanket. The boy continues to query a gray goose about feathers, a red hen about eggs, a yellow bee about honey, and a brown cow about milk. At the end of the day, the boy sings, "Sleep tight, farm friends. May I dream with you?" and they respond, "Yes, sir, yes, sir, yes, please do."

STORYTELLING TIPS: You can sing the entire text even though the lyrics take a turn from the traditional song pattern. The melody can be found on the Internet as well as the following children's music recordings: *Singable Songs for the Very Young* by Raffi (Troubadour, 1976) and *Wee Sing Animals, Animals, Animals* by Pamela Beall and Susan Nipp (Price Stern Sloan, 1999). Simply sing the melody of the first two lines from the traditional song over and over. For example, the first verse goes, "Baa, baa, black sheep, have you any wool? Yes, sir, yes, sir, three bags full." The next lines are "Does wool make a blanket for my bed? Yes, sir, yes, sir, the black sheep said." The text then moves on to the next animal.

Song

"I Had a Rooster," traditional; adapted by Rob Reid.

- -

The melody can be found on the Internet as well as the following children's music recordings: *If I Had a Pony* by Sarah Barchas (High Haven, 1996), *Hello Everybody* by Rachel Buchman (A Gentle Wind, 1986), and *Whaddaya Think of That* by Laurie Berkner (Two Tomatoes, 2000). Berkner's version is titled "I Love My Rooster."

The first verse follows many traditional versions, and I added the newer verses featuring animals and their colors. Make a funny face when you sing the verse about the blue whale. Have the children make the sound effects with you.

I had a rooster, my rooster pleased me,
I fed my rooster 'neath the old chestnut tree,
My little rooster went "Cock-a-doodle-doo,
Dee-doodle-dee-doodle-dee-doodly-do."

I had a green frog, my green frog pleased me,
I fed my green frog 'neath the old chestnut tree,
My little green frog went "Ga-lunk! Ga-lunk!"
My little rooster went "Cock-a-doodle-doo,
Dee-doodle-dee-doodle-dee-doodly-do."

I had a gold snake, my gold snake pleased me,
I fed my gold snake 'neath the old chestnut tree,
My little gold snake went "Slither, slither!"
My little green frog went "Ga-lunk! Ga-lunk!"
My little rooster went "Cock-a-doodle-doo,
Dee-doodle-dee-doodle-dee-doodly-do."

I had a gray goose, my gray goose pleased me,
I fed my gray goose 'neath the old chestnut tree,
My little gray goose went "Honk! Honk!"
My little gold snake went "Slither! Slither!"
My little green frog went "Ga-lunk! Ga-lunk!"

My little rooster went "Cock-a-doodle-doo,
Dee-doodle-dee-doodle-dee-doodly-do."

I had a brown dog, my brown dog pleased me,
I fed my brown dog 'neath the old chestnut tree,
My little brown dog went "Arf! Arf!"
My little gray goose went "Honk! Honk!"
My little gold snake went "Slither! Slither!"
My little green frog went "Ga-lunk! Ga-lunk!"
My little rooster went "Cock-a-doodle-doo,
Dee-doodle-dee-doodle-dee-doodly-do."

I had a white goat, my white goat pleased me,
I fed my white goat 'neath the old chestnut tree,
My little white goat went "Baa! Baa!"
My little brown dog went "Arf! Arf!"
My little gray goose went "Honk! Honk!"
My little gold snake went "Slither! Slither!"
My little green frog went "Ga-lunk! Ga-lunk!"
My little rooster went "Cock-a-doodle-doo,
Dee-doodle-dee-doodle-dee-doodly-do."

I had a pink pig, my pink pig pleased me,
I fed my pink pig 'neath the old chestnut tree,
My little pink pig went "Oink! Oink!"
My little white goat went "Baa! Baa!"
My little brown dog went "Arf! Arf!"
My little gray goose went "Honk! Honk!"
My little gold snake went "Slither! Slither!"
My little green frog went "Ga-lunk! Ga-lunk!"
My little rooster went "Cock-a-doodle-doo,
Dee-doodle-dee-doodle-dee-doodly-do."

I had a black cow, my black cow pleased me,
I fed my black cow 'neath the old chestnut tree,
My little black cow went "Moo! Moo!"

My little pink pig went "Oink! Oink!"
My little white goat went "Baa! Baa!"
My little brown dog went "Arf! Arf!"
My little gray goose went "Honk! Honk!"
My little gold snake went "Slither! Slither!"
My little green frog went "Ga-lunk! Ga-lunk!"
My little rooster went "Cock-a-doodle-doo,
Dee-doodle-dee-doodle-dee-doodly-do."

I had a blue whale, my blue whale pleased me,
I fed my blue whale 'neath the old chestnut tree,
My little blue whale went "There she blows!"
My little black cow went "Moo! Moo!"
My little pink pig went "Oink! Oink!"
My little white goat went "Baa! Baa!"
My little brown dog went "Arf! Arf!"
My little gray goose went "Honk! Honk!"
My little gold snake went "Slither! Slither!"
My little green frog went "Ga-lunk! Ga-lunk!"
My little rooster went "Cock-a-doodle-doo,
Dee-doodle-dee-doodle-dee-doodly-do."

Picture Book

It's an Orange Aardvark! by Michael Hall. Illustrated by the author.
Greenwillow, 2014.

- -

Several ants spot something through the holes in their stump. They
are worried it might be a gray aardvark with a long tongue "perfect
for eating carpenter ants." When they peek, they see the color orange
and panic. "It's an orange aardvark!" They drill another hole and spot
something orange and blue. "It's worse than I thought. It's an orange
aardvark and it's wearing blue pajamas!" Next, they see the color red
and decide the aardvark has a bottle of ketchup. The story line continues with the ants spotting these other colors: green (the aardvark

brought geckos to help eat the ants), yellow (a bulldozer to knock over the stump), and purple (grape juice to wash down the ants). When the ants leave the stump, they spot a rainbow.

STORYTELLING TIPS: As the ants discover each new color, they exclaim "Goodness!," "Gracious!," and "Yikes!" Before reading the story, divide your audience into three groups and assign each group one of those words. As you read the story, point to each group in succession for them to shout out their word. And, of course, wear something orange.

Picture Book

Baby Bear Sees Blue by Ashley Wolff. Illustrated by the author.
Beach Lane, 2012.

When Baby Bear wakes up in his cave, he sees a yellow light outside. His mother tells him it's the sun. Baby Bear and his mother go for a walk. Baby Bear learns about green leaves, blue jays, brown trout, red strawberries, and orange butterflies. When gray clouds accompany thunder and rain, Baby Bear and his mother return to their cave. When the storm is over, they both spot a rainbow. Baby Bear goes to sleep "and sees nothing but deep, soft black."

STORYTELLING TIPS: The pattern of this story repeats the line "Baby Bear sees . . ." and the featured color. As you read, pause after the word "sees" and let the children shout out the correct color.

Closing Creative Dramatics

"Animal Photo Poses" by Rob Reid.

- -

Everyone stands. Inform the children that you are going to take pictures of them with your pretend camera while they make the shapes for different animals. Model the pose for them and then pretend to take their picture as they pose.

Pink flamingo . . . turn head and rest it on shoulder.
Stand on one leg.

Green turtle . . . get on all fours and scrunch head into shoulders.

Gray elephant . . . hold arm upraised in front of nose to represent a trunk.

Blue peacock . . . hold hands behind bottom with thumbs intertwined and fingers extended outward.

Brown moose . . . put thumbs on each side of head with fingers extended outward.

5 Fun Backup Picture Books

Art & Max by David Wiesner. Illustrated by the author. Clarion, 2010.

- -

A lizard named Art is an artist. Another lizard named Max wants to paint, too. Max splashes a variety of colors on Art. The colors then change styles. When Art drinks water, the colors wash away, leaving a line outline of the lizard. Max sprays the colors from a vacuum cleaner to make a new look for Art.

Blue Chameleon by Emily Gravett. Illustrated by the author.
Simon & Schuster, 2010.

- -

A chameleon is lonely. He spots a banana and promptly turns yellow. He sees a cockatoo and turns pink. The chameleon does the same process with a swirly snail, a brown boot, a stripy sock, a spotty ball, a gold fish, a green grasshopper, a gray rock, and a white page. The chameleon finally befriends a multicolored chameleon.

I Know a Wee Piggy by Kim Norman. Illustrated by Henry Cole. Dial, 2012.

- -

A pig at the fair gets covered with a variety of colors in this cumulative text. He wallows in brown mud and then gets covered with red tomatoes, white milk, pink cotton candy, yellow egg yolks, black paint, green grass, and orange clay. He grabs a purple scarf and jumps into blue water (and wins a blue ribbon, too).

Quiet Bunny's Many Colors by Lisa McCue. Illustrated by the author. Sterling, 2011.

- -

Quiet Bunny loves the variety of color in the spring forest. He covers himself with yellow flowers, green lily pads, blueberries, and red clay. When he washes the colors off, the other animals inform him that he is brown and white "and that is why the spring forest is beautiful."

Red Cat Blue Cat by Jenni Desmond. Illustrated by the author. Blue Apple, 2012.

- -

Blue Cat stays upstairs and Red Cat stays downstairs. They don't get along. However, Red Cat secretly "wished he were as smart as Blue Cat and Blue Cat wanted to be fast and bouncy like Red Cat." They try their best to change their colors but these new friends ultimately realize they work best as themselves.

IT'S A SMALL WORLD

STORIES AND ACTIVITIES
ABOUT TINY ANIMALS

★ Opening Picture Book: *Itsy Bitsy Spider* by Richard Egielski

★ Fingerplay: "Spider Here, Spider There" by Rob Reid

★ Picture Book: *Not Inside This House!* by Kevin Lewis and David Ercolini

★ Movement Activity: "This Funny Bug" by Rob Reid

★ Picture Book / Felt and Puppet Story: *Ten Little Caterpillars* by Bill Martin Jr. and Lois Ehlert

★ Picture Book: *Jam & Honey* by Melita Morales and Laura J. Bryant

★ Fingerplay: "A Bee Sat on My Nose," traditional

★ Closing Picture Book: *There Was an Old Lady Who Swallowed Some Bug* by Johnette Downing

Opening Picture Book

Itsy Bitsy Spider by Richard Egielski. Illustrated by the author. Paper engineering by Gene Vosough. Atheneum, 2012.

The itsy bitsy spider wears a red cap and multi-legged overalls in this elaborate paper-engineered pop-up book. The opening pages show our tiny protagonist in front of a large housing complex. We see him entering the bottom of a waterspout when the pages are tucked together. He pokes his head out of the top of the spout when the pages are spread apart. A large cloud releases several anthropomorphic raindrops on the spider while he's on the rooftop. We get a great look inside the bottom of the spout as those raindrops wash "the spider out" and head our way. The sun pops up over the village, and the spider climbs up once again, this time into the outstretched hands of his mother.

> **STORYTELLING TIPS:** Be sure to sing the tune of "The Itsy Bitsy Spider" while you show the pop-up displays. The melody can be found on the Internet as well as the following children's music recordings: *Animal Songs* by Susie Tallman (Rock Me Baby Records, 2012) and *Dana's Best Sing & Play-A-Long Tunes* by Dana Cohenour (Swiggle Ditties, 1995). Sing it very slowly so that the audience members get a good look at the various pop-up images. In fact, because the song is so short, read or sing it a second time and have them join you in song. Don't be surprised if the children automatically chime in during the first time through. Also, read the funny newspaper article on the back cover. "We've got some showers coming our way today, but it won't be a washout."

Fingerplay

"Spider Here, Spider There" by Rob Reid.

Everyone stands. Have children hold up one hand to represent the spider. Have them wiggle their fingers as they move their hands.

Spider here, (*Place hand on one shoulder.*)
Spider there, (*Place hand on other shoulder.*)
This little spider (*Hold hand out front.*)
Is everywhere. (*Place hand all over body rapidly.*)

He's on my knee. (*Hand on knee.*)
He's on my toes. (*Hand on one foot.*)
He's on my belly. (*Hand on belly.*)
He's on my nose. (*Hand on nose.*)

He's on my head. (*Hand on top of head.*)
But then he fled. (*Hold out arm and point toward door.*)
I bet he's off (*Hand over eyes peering in the distance.*)
To spin his web. (*Wiggle fingers on both hands and wave hands around each other.*)

Picture Book

Not Inside This House! by Kevin Lewis. Illustrated by David Ercolini. Orchard, 2011.

- -

A boy named Livingston Columbus Magellan Crous finds ordinary games and toys boring. He'd rather explore and collect the things he finds. When he brings home some bugs, his mother yells, "Livingston Columbus Magellan Crous / I'll have no bugs inside this house / I'll say it once. Won't say it twice / To speak again will not suffice!" He next traps a mouse. His mother goes into a similar rant. Livingston proceeds to bring home a pig, a mouse, an elephant, and a whale. His

STORYTELLING TIPS: Before you turn the page to reveal the next animal Livingston brings home, ask the kids if they can guess what he'll bring home next. Give them the hint that each creature gets bigger and bigger.

poor mother keeps telling him to remove them. When Livingston brings home another bug, "His mother thought. She made a shrug / then gave her son a great big hug / which meant that he could keep the bug."

Movement Activity

"This Funny Bug" by Rob Reid.

Everyone stands. Have the children bend over and point as if seeing something tiny on the ground.

This funny bug
Is a teeny-tiny bug.
I'll give it some food
And a great big hug.
Fun! (*Have everyone straighten up just a little, look straight ahead, and point.*)

This funny bug
Is a medium-sized bug.
I'll give it some food
And a great big hug.
Fun! (*Have everyone look slightly higher and point.*)

This funny bug
Is a great big bug.
I'll give it some food
And a great big hug.
Fun! (*Look straight up overhead and point.*)

This scary bug
Is a HUGE GIGANTIC BUG!
I won't give it food
And I won't give a hug!
RUN!!!

Picture Book / Felt and Puppet Story

Ten Little Caterpillars by Bill Martin Jr. Illustrated by Lois Ehlert.
Beach Lane, 2011.

We meet ten little caterpillars. One by one, they do their own thing. The first one crawls into a bower, and the second one wriggles up a flower. The rhymed text follows them through to the ninth caterpillar that falls into the sea and the tenth one that scales an apple tree. That last caterpillar hangs patiently "until by and by, the tenth caterpillar becomes a butterfly."

> **STORYTELLING TIPS:** Make nine colorful caterpillar shapes out of felt and place them on the felt board one by one. For the last butterfly, pull out the caterpillar puppet and slowly, before the children's eyes, transform it into a butterfly. The Folkmanis puppet company makes the reversible puppet.

Picture Book

Jam & Honey by Melita Morales. Illustrated by Laura J. Bryant.
Tricycle Press, 2011.

A little girl accompanies her mother to the park. The girl picks berries but is frightened by a bee. She stands very still and knows that by doing so "there's nothing to fear." The bee moves on, and the girl heads back home with her mother and a bucket of berries. The story starts over from the bee's perspective. It heads to the park and is surprised by the girl. The bee is scared but quietly moves away. It

> **STORYTELLING TIPS:** This is a nice, quiet book. With both story lines, read the narrative with a nice, even flow. Stop short with a surprised "OH!" when the girl spots the bee and again when the bee sees the girl.

heads home to make honey. The final illustration shows the girl eating bread with jam and honey and the bee flying in the background.

Fingerplay

"A Bee Sat on My Nose," traditional.

- -

What do you suppose?
A bee sat on my nose. (*Place finger on nose.*)
Then what do you think?
He gave me a wink. (*Wink.*)
And said, "I beg your pardon!
I thought you were a garden!" (*Have finger "fly" away like a bee.*)
Bzzzzzz!

Closing Picture Book

There Was an Old Lady Who Swallowed Some Bug by Johnette Downing. Illustrated by the author. Pelican, 2010.

- -

There was an old lady who swallowed a fly. We see a close-up of the old lady's mouth and tongue along with her stomach as she swallows

> **STORYTELLING TIPS:** Sing the text to tune of the traditional song "I Know an Old Lady Who Swallowed a Fly." The melody can be found on the Internet as well as the following children's music recordings: *Travel Song Sing-Alongs* by Kevin Roth (Marlboro, 1994) and *Peter, Paul & Mommy Too* by Peter, Paul, and Mary (Warner Brothers, 1993). Encourage the kids to make disgusting noises as you mention each critter going down her throat. Pause before the end when you read "She . . . CROAKED!" and turn the page to show the old lady's frog identity. This book might also lend itself to being presented as a felt-board story. Make a felt stomach and felt pieces for each of the creatures mentioned. Place the creatures inside the stomach one by one.

the fly, a spider, a flea, an ant, a slug, a worm, a mosquito, and a roach to the rhythm of the traditional song. The kids will be surprised at the last picture when they learn that the old lady is a frog.

5 Fun Backup Picture Books

The Ant and the Grasshopper by Rebecca Emberley and Ed Emberley. Illustrated by the authors. Roaring Brook, 2012.

- -

Ant is working hard to drag "the remnants of a picnic" but is exhausted by the work. She hears some music and heads toward the sound. She sees a "grasshopper and his band making music with complete abandon." The ant is rejuvenated by the music. The band follows the ant back to her colony. "Come on everybody, we're going underground!" They do so and make everything brighter.

The Flea by Laurie Cohen. Illustrated by Marjorie Béal. Owl Kids, 2014.

- -

A tiny flea thinks that he's too little. He climbs up on top of a pea, an apple, a flower, a plant, a tree, a house, telephone wires, a skyscraper, "and finally up, up, up on a cloud." A bear spots the flea and shouts, "You're not big at all. You're teeny-tiny!" The flea jumps down on the bear. After scratching all over, the bear realizes that the flea is indeed big: "A big nuisance."

How to Teach a Slug to Read by Susan Pearson. Illustrated by David Slonim. Marshall Cavendish, 2011.

- -

The narrator gives us some helpful tips in our quest to teach a slug how to read. Those hints include putting written labels on his favorite things (beans, carrots, and bugs) and finding a really good book (*Rhymes from Mother Slug* and *A Tale of Two Termites*). We also see slug versions of classic children's books: *The Poky Little Slug, Go Slug Go,* and *Where the Wild Slugs Are.* Eventually, the slug "may start a story hour or even a school," thanks to you.

Scritch-Scratch a Perfect Match by Kimberly Marcus. Illustrated by Mike Lester. Putnam, 2011.

A tiny flea starts pestering a dog. "'AAROOF!' howled the stray as he jumped in the air. AWOOMPH was the sound as he dropped like a sack landing THUD! 'OH CRUD!' on an old man's back." The now muddy dog and man run into a store. The dog runs over to a can of flea powder on the shelf. The man grabs the can, and the two head outside. The flea jumps off the dog and onto a cat. The dog and man head off into the sunset while the cat races for the store.

Snippet the Early Riser by Bethanie Deeney Murguia. Illustrated by the author. Knopf, 2013.

Snippet the snail always woke up earlier than the rest of his family. "'Hmph. How did I end up with a family of slugs?' wondered Snippet." Grasshopper helps Snippet jump on the snails' bed, which is really a leaf. Cricket helps make music to wake up Snippet's family. "Mama wheezed. Sister snuffled. But still, no one came out to play." After several insects turn down Stinkbug's offer to "stink them out," Snippet gathers several leaves to serve as breakfast. The sweet smell of the leaves finally wakes up the rest of the family.

BIG AND TALL

STORIES AND ACTIVITIES
ABOUT LARGE ANIMALS

- -

Opening Picture Book

A Big Guy Took My Ball! by Mo Willems. Illustrated by the author. Hyperion, 2013.

Piggie is upset because a big guy took her ball. Her friend Gerald the elephant is outraged and heads off to recover Piggie's ball from the big guy. Gerald is stunned to see that the big guy is an enormous whale. He slowly retreats and tells Piggie, "That is a BIG guy. You did not say *how* big he was. He is very BIG." The whale approaches the two friends and is upset that no one will play with him because of his big size. Piggie and Gerald invent a game they call "Whale Ball," and the three new friends have "BIG FUN!"

> **STORYTELLING TIPS:** Gerald's lines are particularly fun to read aloud. At first he's outraged. "Big guys have *all* the fun!" even though he himself is a big guy. After encountering the whale for the first time, Gerald is excited and distraught. "'He is so BIGGY-BIG-BIG!'" Read the whale's lines in your deepest voice. Bring it down to a whisper when he says, "Little guys have *all* the fun."

Fingerplay

"Over in the Creek" by Rob Reid.

Sing to the tune of the first part of the traditional song "Over in the Meadow." The melody can be found on the Internet as well as the following children's music recordings: *Animal Songs* by Susie Tallman (Rock Me Baby Records, 2012) and *Wee Sing Nursery Rhymes and Lullabies* by Pamela Beall and Susan Nipp (Price Stern Sloan, 1985). Before sharing this "tiny to gigantic" rhyme with the children, explain what a "musky," or muskellunge, fish is. Show them a picture if you have one. Also, explain the term "gulf."

Over in the creek,
Swimming all around,
(*Place both hands together and make swimming motions.*)
Swam a tiny minnow,
(*Make an "inch" length with thumb and pointer finger.*)
Moving up and down. (*Resume swimming motions.*)

Over in the pond,
Swimming all around,
(*Place both hands together and make swimming motions.*)
Swam a little sunfish,
(*Make a "foot-length" measurement with both hands.*)
Moving up and down. (*Resume swimming motions.*)

Over in the lake,
Swimming all around,
(*Place both hands together and make swimming motions.*)
Swam a good-sized musky,
(*Make a "yard-length" measurement with both hands.*)
Moving up and down. (*Resume swimming motions.*)

Over in the gulf,
Swimming all around,
(*Place both hands together and make swimming motions.*)
Swam a great big shark, (*Spread both arms as wide apart as possible.*)
Moving up and down. (*Resume swimming motions.*)

Over in the ocean,
Swimming all around,
(*Place both hands together and make swimming motions.*)
Swam a gigantic whale,
(*Place hand over eyes as if looking in the distance.*)
Moving up and down. (*Resume swimming motions.*)

Picture Book

Boa's Bad Birthday by Jeanne Willis. Illustrated by Tony Ross. Lerner, 2014.

Boas are among the largest snakes in the world. Young Boa is looking forward to his birthday presents from his friends. Unfortunately, the presents are all inappropriate. Orangutan brought Boa an enormous piano, but "Boa couldn't play it. He had no fingers." Monkey gave a pair of sunglasses for Boa's gift, but "they kept slipping off. He had no ears or nose." Jaguar brings mittens (Boa has no hands), Sloth brings a hairbrush (Boa has no hair), Anteater brings a soccer ball (Boa has no feet), and Dung Beetle brings, well, "you know what." However, a tree grows from the dung ball. "It was the perfect present for a boa."

STORYTELLING TIPS: Boa finds out about each inappropriate gift with a page turn. Build up the excitement at the thought of each new gift, pause, turn the page, and then reflect the letdown with your voice.

Picture Book

Jangles: A Big Fish Story by David Shannon. Illustrated by the author. Scholastic, 2012.

Jangles, the largest fish around, got his name from the many lures and fishhooks stuck in his jaw. "Jangles was so big, he ate eagles from trees that hung over the lake and full-grown beavers that strayed too far from home." He also rescued little children who fell into the lake. One day, the narrator's father hooks Jangles and is pulled down deep "into the cold, black lake." He learns that Jangles is not only a fish but also a storyteller. And with this tall tale, the narrator's father is a storyteller, too.

Fingerplay

"Jangles the Fish," traditional; adapted by Rob Reid.

This fingerplay was inspired by both the David Shannon book and the camp favorite "Hermie the Worm."

> I was fishing in my boat, (*Mime holding a "fishing pole."*)
> Woo-woo, (*Bob the "fishing pole" up and down.*)
> Chewing my bubble gum,
> Chew, chew, chew, (*Make exaggerated chewing motions.*)
> When along swam Jangles the fish.
> (*Make swimming motions with hands.*)
> And he was *this* big. (*Hold up fingers an inch apart.*)
> And I said, "Jangles! What happened?" (*Hold up hands, palms up.*)
> He said, "I ate a worm."
>
> I was fishing in my boat, (*Mime holding a "fishing pole."*)
> Woo-woo, (*Bob the "fishing pole" up and down.*)
> Chewing my bubble gum,
> Chew, chew, chew, (*Make exaggerated chewing motions.*)
> When along swam Jangles the fish.
> (*Make swimming motions with hands.*)
> And he was *this* big. (*Hold up fingers two inches apart.*)
> And I said, "Jangles! What happened?" (*Hold up hands, palms up.*)
> He said, "I ate a minnow."
>
> I was fishing in my boat, (*Mime holding a "fishing pole."*)
> Woo-woo, (*Bob the "fishing pole" up and down.*)
> Chewing my bubble gum,
> Chew, chew, chew, (*Make exaggerated chewing motions.*)
> When along swam Jangles the fish.
> (*Make swimming motions with hands.*)
> And he was *this* big. (*Hold up hands six inches apart.*)
> And I said, "Jangles! What happened?" (*Hold up hands, palms up.*)
> He said, "I ate a frog."

I was fishing in my boat, (*Mime holding a "fishing pole."*)

Woo-woo, (*Bob the "fishing pole" up and down.*)

Chewing my bubble gum,

Chew, chew, chew, (*Make exaggerated chewing motions.*)

When along swam Jangles the fish.

(*Make swimming motions with hands.*)

And he was *this* big. (*Hold up hands as far apart as possible.*)

And I said, "Jangles! What happened?" (*Hold up hands, palms up.*)

He said, "I ate a whale."

I was fishing in my boat, (*Mime holding a "fishing pole."*)

Woo-woo, (*Bob the "fishing pole" up and down.*)

Chewing my bubble gum,

Chew, chew, chew, (*Make exaggerated chewing motions.*)

When along swam Jangles the fish.

(*Make swimming motions with hands.*)

And he was *this* big. (*Hold up thumb and index finger an inch apart.*)

And I said, "Jangles! What happened?" (*Hold up hands, palms up.*)

He said, "I burped."

Picture Book

Big and Small by Elizabeth Bennett. Illustrated by Jane Chapman.
Tiger Tales, 2014.

- -

A big bear named Big is good friends with a small mouse named Small.
While playing, Small stubs his toe and says, "A little help, please!" Big

STORYTELLING TIPS: Inform your audience ahead of time that a small mouse named Small will say "A little help, please!" four times in the story. Have the kids practice those lines in small, high-pitched voices, and ask them to recite the lines at the proper times in the story. Let them know that a bear named Big will say those same lines at the end of the story and to practice with big, deep voices.

helps out. When the two cross a stream, Small becomes stranded. Big helps out once again. Next, Small is frightened by a bee. Big protects his little friend. Small then tumbles down a hole, and Big pulls him out. That evening, Big has trouble falling asleep. He needs a hug. He pleads, "A little help, please!" Small helps out.

Picture Book

The Short Giraffe by Neil Flory. Illustrated by Mark Cleary. Albert Whitman, 2014.

Baboon is taking a photo of the giraffes, "the tallest animals in the world." However, Geri the giraffe is so short that he is barely visible in the picture. The other giraffes come up with ideas to make Geri taller. They tied stilts to his legs, they stacked him on turtles, they hung him upside down from a tree, they filled him with helium, and they attached fake wings to him. "They even tried springs but Geri just bounced and bounced and bounced all around." A tiny caterpillar suggests that instead of making Geri taller, the other giraffes bend down to Geri's size.

> **STORYTELLING TIPS:** Read the caterpillar's voice in a high-pitched manner. At the end of the story, have your audience members crowd around each other, similar to how the giraffes loop around each other to be similar heights, and take a picture of the kids (or even a pretend picture).

Closing Musical Activity

"Five Tall Giraffes" by Colleen Hannafin and B. Squat Woody.

Everyone stands. Sing to the tune of the traditional song "My Darling Clementine." The song can be found on the children's music recording *Shake It Down, Turn Around* by Colleen and Uncle Squaty (North Side Music, 2010).

One giraffe, with his long neck, (*Lift head to show neck.*)
Stretched to touch the sky so blue. (*Point chin to ceiling.*)
Called another giraffe to join him,
(*Beckon to an unseen friend to join you.*)
All together there were two. (*Hold up two fingers.*)

Two giraffes, with their long tongues, (*Stick out tongue.*)
Plucked the leaves from the thorny tree. (*Pretend to eat.*)
Called another giraffe to join them,
(*Beckon to an unseen friend to join you.*)
All together there were three. (*Hold up three fingers.*)

Three giraffes, spread their long legs,
(*Spread legs apart, bend at waist, and lower head.*)
To drink the water along the shore. (*Mime lapping up water with tongue.*)
Called another giraffe to join them,
(*Beckon to an unseen friend to join you.*)
All together there were four. (*Hold up four fingers.*)

Four giraffes, long eyelashes, (*Blink eyes.*)
To keep the sand out of their eyes. (*Sweep eyes with hand.*)
Called another giraffe to join them,
(*Beckon to an unseen friend to join you.*)
All together there were five. (*Hold up five fingers.*)

All giraffes have long eyelashes, (*Point to eyelashes.*)
Long legs and necks and tongues. (*Point to legs, neck, and tongue.*)
So we've learned through the song we're singing,
Many parts of the giraffe are long. (*Stretch upward as high as possible.*)

5 Fun Backup Picture Books

The Crocodile and the Scorpion by Rebecca Emberley and Ed Emberley. Illustrated by the authors. Roaring Brook, 2013.

- -

Crocodile's appetite was very large and his brain was very small. Scorpion's "stinger was very sharp, but his mind was not." Scorpion asks Crocodile to carry him across the river. Crocodile agrees to do so as long as Scorpion doesn't sting him. Scorpion agrees and Crocodile promises not to bite Scorpion. In the middle of the river, Scorpion stings Crocodile. Crocodile in turn lunges at Scorpion. They argue all the way to the bottom of the river.

Hiding Phil by Eric Barclay. Illustrated by the author. Scholastic, 2013.

- -

Three children find an elephant by a bus stop. The elephant's suitcase has the name Phil on it. The children play jump rope, go on the teeter-totter, and swim with Phil. The kids decide they need to hide Phil, but he's too big. When the parents discover Phil, they state, "We have to take him back where you found him." At the last minute, the parents change their minds, and Phil stays with the children.

Hippospotamus by Jeanne Willis. Illustrated by Tony Ross. Lerner, 2012.

- -

A hippopotamus is worried by a red spot on her behind. She "had a **spot**amus . . . on her bottomus." Weasel thinks its measles, Fox declares "it's hippopox," Beaver believes it's jungle fever, Lion thinks it's "hippolumps," Shrew says "potomumps," and Rhino says "hippo-flu." Other characters suggest the spot is a blister, an ingrown hair, and an allergic reaction. Finally, a human child walks by and plucks off the red spot because the spot is actually the child's missing bubble gum.

My Rhinoceros by Jon Agee. Illustrated by the author. Scholastic, 2011.

- -

A boy buys a large rhinoceros at a pet store. "I didn't really know what I was getting into." The boy is disappointed his rhino won't fetch balls, sticks, or Frisbees. "He didn't roll over. He didn't do anything." A rhinoceros expert informs the boy that rhinos only "pop balloons and poke holes in kites." The boy thinks that perhaps he should have bought a hippopotamus instead. While the boy is walking his rhinoceros in the park, a bank robbery occurs, with one robber getting away in a hot air balloon and another escaping in a kite. Of course, the rhinoceros pops the hot air balloon, pokes a hole in the kite, and saves the day.

Tug-of-War by John Burningham. Illustrated by the author. Candlewick, 2013.

Hare is constantly being teased by the much larger Hippopotamus and Elephant. "What a tiny, wimpy thing you are, with those ridiculous ears." Hare challenges Elephant to a duel of tug-of-war. He gives Elephant one end of the rope and heads down to the river where he challenges Hippopotamus as well. Elephant and Hippopotamus have no idea they are pulling against each other. "Elephant felt the pull on the rope and was amazed at the strength of Hare. Hippopotamus could not believe how hard Hare was pulling the rope." When the two large creatures realize they have been tricked, they search high and low for Hare. But Hare has already made his escape.

DEEP DOWN UNDERGROUND

STORIES AND ACTIVITIES ABOUT ANIMALS
THAT LIVE BELOW THE GROUND

PROGRAM AT A GLANCE

- ★ Opening Picture Book: *Underground* by Denise Fleming

- ★ Picture Book: *Goldie and the Three Hares* by Margie Palatini and Jack E. Davis

- ★ Song: "Little Skunk's Hole," traditional

- ★ Picture Book: *Digger Dog* by William Bee and Cecilia Johansson

- ★ Movement Activity: "Dig-a-Dig-a-Dig-a-Dig-a" by Rob Reid

- ★ Picture Book: *Oh, No!* by Candace Fleming and Eric Rohmann

- ★ Closing Movement Activity: "We're Going to Explore a Cave," traditional; adapted by Rob Reid

Opening Picture Book

Underground by Denise Fleming. Illustrated by the author.
Beach Lane, 2012.

While a little boy helps plant a cherry tree, we are able to see underground activity that includes a shrew, a mole, ants, grubs, and more. Through cross-section illustrations, we also see a dog burying a bone, a robin grabbing an earthworm, chipmunks traveling through underground "highways and byways," and a turtle laying eggs. Many other animals are captured in their underground lifestyles. Finally, we see the underground depiction of the planted tree before the above-ground view of animals poking their heads up to see the departing boy and his dog.

> **STORYTELLING TIPS:** Before starting the story, use the question found on the front jacket flap as your introduction: "Do you ever wonder what creatures live under the dirt beneath your feet?" Ask the kids what kind of animals live underground. Each double-page spread contains just a few words. The first spread has "Low down" and the second reads "Way down." Some are a delight to read aloud: "Squirm-ways and worm-ways." Pace yourself with a slow, quiet delivery. Add a long pause between each phrase to allow the children to take in all the action found in the illustrations. At the end of the book, Denise Fleming provides a "Creature Identification" feature. Point to one, such as the yellow jacket nest, and ask the kids if they saw that picture in the book. Flip back and forth to find where the yellow jackets appeared. Do this with a few more creatures before moving on to the next picture book.

Picture Book

Goldie and the Three Hares by Margie Palatini. Illustrated by Jack E. Davis.
Katherine Tegan Books, 2011.

In this retelling of "Goldilocks and the Three Bears," the Hare family is "enjoying a quiet, peaceful, lovely day at home down their rabbit hole" when they hear a "Thump, Bump, Kaboom. Kaboom. Kaboom!" While running away from three bears, Goldilocks has fallen into the rabbit hole and sprained her foot. Papa Hare, Mama Hare, and Baby Hare try to nurse her back to health, but that proves difficult. Goldilocks complains that the first chair they sit her down in is too hard, the second chair too soft, and the third chair? "Don't even go there! I'll take the couch!" The Hares finally get rid of their rude guest when they mention inviting the Bears over for a visit. Before the Hares can fully relax, another girl falls down their hole and asks, "I say, has anyone seen a white rabbit lately?"

STORYTELLING TIPS: Have a lot of fun sharing the bossiness of Goldilocks through her lines. Deliver them loudly: "Hey! I need a pillow here! Now! Quick like a bunny—and remember, not too hard. Not too soft. Just right . . . And get one for my foot, too."

Song

"Little Skunk's Hole," traditional.

- -

Versions of this traditional camp song can be found on the following children's music recordings: *Wee Sing Animals, Animals, Animals* (Price Stern Sloan, 1999) and *Wee Sing Silly Songs* (Price Stern Sloan, 1982), both by Pamela Beall and Susan Nipp. Make a circle with your hands to frame your head. On the skunk's repeated lines of "Take it out," wag your finger. On the line "Pee-uuu," roll your eyes, pinch your nose, and fan the air with your hand.

> Well, I stuck my head in a little skunk's hole,
> And the little skunk said "Well, bless my soul!
> Take it out!
> Take it out!
> Remove it!"
> But, I didn't take it out,
> And the little skunk said "If you don't take it out,

You'll wish you had.
Take it out!
Take it out!
Remove it!"
Pee-uuu!
I removed it!

Picture Book

Digger Dog by William Bee. Illustrated by Cecilia Johansson.
Candlewick, 2013.

- -

Digger Dog loves to dig for bones. He sniffs them out and starts digging with a shovel. "But the ground is too hard and the bone is too deep." Digger Dog uses a digger machine, "but the ground is still too hard and the bone is still too deep." The pattern continues as Digger Dog gets a bigger digger, "a much bigger digger," and finally (as a lift-the-flap feature reveals), the biggest digger in the world. More flaps reveal the world's biggest bone. The final flap cutaway scene reveals a complete dinosaur skeleton still buried in the ground.

STORYTELLING TIPS: When Digger Dog sniffs for bones, ask the kids in the audience to sniff along. After you read the phrase "But the ground is too hard and the bone is too deep" the first time, cue your audience members to recite it with you. The second time, pause before the word "hard" and let them say it. Pause before the word "deep" and they will chime in with that word, too. After that, they will know to recite the entire phrase with you. Play up the drama at the end when you manipulate each folding page. Every single time I've shared this book with kids, there is an audible "Whoa!" as they first see the size of the world's largest digger, then the world's largest bone, and, finally, the dinosaur skeleton.

Movement Activity

"Dig-a-Dig-a-Dig-a-Dig-a" by Rob Reid.

Have the children stand and mime digging a hole with a shovel. With every "Dig-a," they will alternate between a downward motion of the shovel scooping dirt and an upward motion of tossing the dirt over their shoulder. Clap once on "Hole!" Perform this routine slowly to allow them to get into the flow of the movements. When you get to the section that goes "A . . . Deeper, Deeper, Deeper, Deeper, Deeper, Deeper Hole!" have the children stand straight up and then slowly bend over on each "Deeper." Again, clap once on "Hole!" They stand straight up and bend over a second time before going back to the first set of motions. If the kids pick up the rhythm of the actions quickly, do the entire activity a second time, but faster.

> Let's . . . Dig-a, Dig-a, Dig-a, Dig-a, Dig-a, Dig-a Hole!
> Let's . . . Dig-a, Dig-a, Dig-a, Dig-a, Dig-a, Dig-a Hole!
> A . . . Deeper, Deeper, Deeper, Deeper, Deeper, Deeper Hole!
> A . . . Deeper, Deeper, Deeper, Deeper, Deeper, Deeper Hole!
> Let's . . . Dig-a, Dig-a, Dig-a, Dig-a, Dig-a, Dig-a Hole!
> Let's . . . Dig-a, Dig-a, Dig-a, Dig-a, Dig-a, Dig-a Hole!

Picture Book

Oh, No! by Candace Fleming. Illustrated by Eric Rohmann. Schwartz & Wade, 2012.

> While fleeing from Tiger, Frog falls into a deep, deep hole with a "Ribbit-oops! Ribbit-oops!" When Mouse tries to pull Frog out, she falls in. They are followed by a procession of animals—Loris, Sun Bear, and Monkey—each with its own accompanying sound effect. Tiger looks down the hole, licking his lips, when the earth starts shaking with a "Ba-Boom! Ba-Boom!" Elephant arrives, knocks Tiger into the hole, and rescues the other animals with his trunk.

Closing Movement Activity

"We're Going to Explore a Cave," traditional; adapted by Rob Reid.

Everyone stands. This activity is based on the traditional story program activity "We're Going on a Bear Hunt."

We're going to explore a cave today,
We're going to explore a cave.
Let's go! (*Slap legs for a few seconds to indicate walking and then stop.*)
It's dark in here.
Turn on your lights. (*Mime turning on headlamps.*)
We're going to explore a cave today, (*Slap legs.*)
We're going to explore a cave. (*Stop slapping.*)
Careful! Tight squeeze. Go sideways. (*Turn sideways and shuffle a few steps to mime squeezing through a narrow passage.*)
We're going to explore a cave today, (*Slap legs.*)
We're going to explore a cave. (*Stop slapping.*)
Look there! Underground pond. Let's swim.
(*Make swimming motions.*)
We're going to explore a cave today, (*Slap legs.*)
We're going to explore a cave. (*Stop slapping.*)
Watch out! Low ceiling. Down on your hands and knees. (*Crawl.*)
We're going to explore a cave today, (*Slap legs.*)
We're going to explore a cave. (*Stop slapping.*)
Wow! A big room. (*Gaze around.*)

What's that flapping sound? (*Hold hand to ear.*)

BATS! (*Make a frightened face and swat "bats" away from head.*)

Let's get out of here! (*Slap legs.*)

Low ceiling! (*Crawl and then stand and slap legs.*)

Underground pond! (*Make swimming motions and then slap legs.*)

Tight squeeze! (*Shuffle sideways and then slap legs.*)

We're out! (*Raise hands in triumph.*)

Turn off your lights. (*Mime turning off lights.*)

Oh look! The bats followed us. (*Point.*)

They're catching bugs. (*Continue pointing.*)

Bye bats! (*Wave.*)

Bye cave! (*Wave.*)

We explored a cave today. (*Point to self proudly.*)

We explored a cave.

Whew! (*Wipe forehead with sleeve.*)

5 Fun Backup Picture Books

***And Then It's Spring* by Julie Fogliano.
Illustrated by Erin E. Stead. Roaring Brook, 2012.**

- -

A young boy plants seeds while the world is brown. He is accompanied by a dog, a turtle, and a rabbit. After a while, the boy starts worrying about the seeds. He's worried about the birds going after the seeds. He even worries about bears. "Because bears can't read signs that say things like 'please do not stomp here—these are seeds and they are trying.'" At one point, we see a nice cross-section of ants, worms, mice, and chipmunks underground. We also see the seeds taking root, although the boy cannot. Finally, the world turns green.

***Diary of a Baby Wombat* by Jackie French.
Illustrated by Bruce Whatley. Clarion, 2010.**

- -

We meet a baby wombat who tells us she lives in a hole in the ground in Australia. On Monday, the baby wombat leaves its hole and meets a human baby. On Tuesday, the two babies play again, and the human baby follows the baby wombat to the hole. On Wednesday and Thursday, Mum wombat looks for a bigger hole. The two babies play and discover different kinds of holes. On Friday, the two babies look at a "GIANT hole!" On Saturday, the wombats move into the human's house. All three sleep on Sunday.

Lucky Ducklings by Eva Moore. Illustrated by Nancy Carpenter. Orchard, 2013.

- -

Mama Duck led her five ducklings on a walk to the park. The ducklings' names were Pippin, Bippin, Tippin, Dippin, and Little Joe. Unfortunately, the ducklings all fell into a storm drain. Mama Duck chased people away from the drain. "'Whack! Whack!' she said. 'Get away from my babies!'" Three firefighters arrived, but the drain cover was stuck. A man named Perry attached a cable to the grate and popped it off. "Fireman Paul climbed down, down into the storm drain." One by one the ducklings were rescued. Mama Duck finally got her babies back.

Over and Under the Snow by Kate Messner. Illustrated by Christopher Silas Neal. Chronicle, 2011.

- -

A girl and her father ski through the woods "frosted fresh and white." When a red squirrel disappears down a crack, Dad informs his daughter that under the snow there is "a whole secret kingdom, where the smallest forest animals stay safe and warm." While the girl and her father continue on, we see a shrew, field mice, voles, a snowshoe hare, bullfrogs, a chipmunk, a beaver, bees, and even a bear living underground.

Who's There? by Carole Lexa Schaefer. Illustrated by Pierr Morgan. Viking, 2011.

A young bunny climbs into bed deep down in the family's underground home. He (or she) hears a "Creak, Creak, Crinch" and wonders "Who's There?" The bunny hears the noise near its cave-like bedroom and imagines terrible creatures such as a Crusty Dumply Ogre, a Grimy Gooey Ghoulie, a Splitch-kah-doo-mee Grabber, and a Two-Headed Whiney Snoop. The bunny turns on a flashlight and sees . . . "my little brother." The creak-creak noises actually come from the little brother's "Pull Duck."

WAY UP HIGH

STORIES AND ACTIVITIES ABOUT
ANIMALS IN THE SKY AND TALL TREES

Opening Picture Book

Peepsqueak! by Leslie Ann Clark. Illustrated by the author.
HarperCollins, 2012.

- -

While the other chicks were slowly waking up, Peepsqueak was "on the move!" More than anything else, Peepsqueak wanted to "fly . . . HIGH!" He ignored the farm animals who told him, "Don't even try. You can't fly high." Peepsqueak tried flying off the top of a wall, a round hill, a stack of chicks, and a rock. Each time, Peepsqueak "fell down, down, down into the soft green grass." Finally, Old Gray Goose took Peepsqueak for a ride "High High High."

STORYTELLING TIPS: The children can chime in on the following repetitive phrases: "He was on the move" and "Peepsqueak jumped UP, UP, UP! And then he fell DOWN, DOWN, DOWN into the soft green grass."

Picture Book

Ol' Mama Squirrel by David Ezra Stein. Illustrated by the author.
Nancy Paulsen, 2013.

- -

Ol' Mama Squirrel protects her babies from "creatures that would love to snack on a baby squirrel" by keeping them safe up high in a tree. When a cat approaches the tree, Ol' Mama Squirrel goes into action by shouting, "Chook, chook, chook! Get away from my babies! Chook, chook, chook! Get out of my tree!" She successfully chases

STORYTELLING TIPS: Before you read the book, teach the children the sound that Ol' Mama Squirrel makes: "Chook, chook, chook!" Whenever she makes the noise in the book, read the line and pause so that the kids can repeat the sound. Encourage them to *shout* those sounds when the one hundred other mama squirrels arrive.

away the cat, an owl, a dog, kites, airplanes, and "the man who came to prune the tree." One day, a grizzly bear proves to be too big of a match for Ol' Mama Squirrel. She raises an alarm from the top of the tree with the cry "Chook, chook, chook!" and one hundred mama squirrels arrive to drive off the bear.

Movement / Sound Effects Activity

"I Spy Way up High," traditional; adapted by Rob Reid.

- -

This activity follows the pattern of the traditional game "I Spy." Inform your young audience that they will be looking for things normally found by looking "way up high."

I spy with my little eye (*Look around.*)
Something special way up high. (*Look up.*)
What's on that tree? (*Point up.*)
It's a squirrel!
Chook-chook-chook! (*Make the squirrel noise.*)

I spy with my little eye (*Look around.*)
Something special way up high. (*Look up.*)
What's on that other tree? (*Point up.*)
It's a woodpecker!
Rat-a-tat-tat! (*Make the woodpecker sound.*)

I spy with my little eye (*Look around.*)
Something special way up high. (*Look up.*)
What's on that mountain? (*Point up.*)
It's a mountain goat!
Bleat! Bleat! (*Make the mountain goat noise.*)

I spy with my little eye (*Look around.*)
Something special way up high. (*Look up.*)
What's in the air? (*Point up.*)

It's an eagle!

Scree! Scree! (*Make the eagle noise.*)

Picture Book

Too Tall Houses **by Gianna Marino. Illustrated by the author. Viking, 2012.**

Rabbit and Owl were good friends, and they each had a small house on top of a hill. Rabbit grew vegetables, and Owl enjoyed his view of the forest. When Rabbit's garden grew tall and blocked Owl's view, "Owl began to build his house taller." Owl's house blocked the sun from reaching the garden, so Rabbit, too, built a taller house. The two former friends kept building and building until "they had the two tallest houses in the world." A strong wind blew their houses down to a pile of twigs and dirt. The two became friends once more and lived together in one small house.

> **STORYTELLING TIPS:** As the two houses grow taller and taller, add more energy and excitement to your voice. Slow down and pause at the double-page spread of the two homes in the atmosphere towering over the planet down below. Read the last phrase—"to build one small house"—slowly, one word at a time.

Fingerplay

"Five Little Monkeys Jumping Oh-So High," traditional; adapted by Rob Reid.

Five little monkeys jumping on the bed, (*Hold up five fingers on one hand and bounce that hand on the palm of the other hand.*)
One bounced higher, "Watch!" she said.
(*Hold up one finger and raise it overhead.*)
That little monkey jumped oh-so high,
She disappeared into the sky!
(*Peer upward with hand shading eyes. Shrug.*)

Four little monkeys jumping on the bed, (*Hold up four fingers on one hand and bounce that hand on the palm of the other hand.*)
One bounced higher, "Watch!" he said.
(*Hold up one finger and raise it overhead.*)
That little monkey jumped oh-so high,
He disappeared into the sky!
(*Peer upward with hand shading eyes. Shrug.*)

Three little monkeys jumping on the bed, (*Hold up three fingers on one hand and bounce that hand on the palm of the other hand.*)
One bounced higher, "Watch!" she said.
(*Hold up one finger and raise it overhead.*)
That little monkey jumped oh-so high,
She disappeared into the sky!
(*Peer upward with hand shading eyes. Shrug.*)

Two little monkeys jumping on the bed, (*Hold up two fingers on one hand and bounce that hand on the palm of the other hand.*)
One bounced higher, "Watch!" he said.
(*Hold up one finger and raise it overhead.*)
That little monkey jumped oh-so high,
He disappeared into the sky!
(*Peer upward with hand shading eyes. Shrug.*)

One little monkey jumping on the bed, (*Hold up one finger on one hand and bounce that hand on the palm of the other hand.*)
One bounced higher, "Watch!" she said.
(*Hold up the finger and raise it overhead.*)
That little monkey jumped oh-so high,
She disappeared into the sky!
(*Peer upward with hand shading eyes. Shrug.*)

No little monkeys jumping on the bed,
(*Look around and shrug shoulders.*)
If you look hard and lift your head, (*Look upward.*)

You'll see a speck below the moon,
Those monkeys hitched a ride in a hot air balloon!
(*Point with a big smile.*)

Picture Book

Millie and the Big Rescue by Alexander Steffensmeier. Illustrated by the author. Bloomsbury, 2012.

- -

Millie the cow finds the best hiding place during a farmyard game of hide-and-seek: the top of a tree. When nobody is able to find Millie, she decides to come down but learns that going up is easier than climbing down. Millie is stuck way up in the tree. The goat spots Millie and quickly climbs up. Soon, all of the other farm animals find ways to climb up to the top of the tree. "Before long, Millie had A LOT of company." The farmer climbs a ladder up into the tree, but she too gets stuck when the ladder falls. She ties a note to a chicken and sends it to the neighbor's house. The neighbor calls the fire department. "'We've rescued several cats from trees,' said the firefighter. 'But a whole farm? That's a new one.'" Everyone decides to have a picnic in the tree.

> **STORYTELLING TIPS:** The various farm animals do many silly things in the background. Don't worry about interrupting the flow of the story line if you pause to point out some of these wacky antics. For example, one chicken is lying under a tractor like a mechanic. Another chicken is eating from a bag of popcorn as she watches other animals propelled into the tree. The dog is wearing the firefighter's hat, and the baby chicks are everywhere.

Picture Book

Up, Tall and High! by Ethan Long. Illustrated by the author. Putnam, 2012.

- -

A variety of birds discuss the concepts of tall, high, and up. In the first short story, a foldout page reveals that the shortest bird is now the tallest with the help of stilts. In the second story, a penguin laments that it cannot go high "because I cannot fly!" The foldout page shows the penguin flying high by holding several helium-filled balloons. In the last story, a bird brags that it is up in the tree and that the other bird is down. When the other bird flies up to the tree, it proudly proclaims, "Now I am up, too!" The foldout page shows the tree collapsing from the weight of the birds. Other birds arrive and say, "We'll help you up!"

STORYTELLING TIPS: The foldout pages add to the fun. Of course, the kids in the audience will want to flip the pages for you. If I have a large group, I usually walk around with this book and let several hands flip the pages together.

Closing Movement Activity

"Flap Your Wings" by Rob Reid.

- -

Flap your wings, (*Flap arms.*)
It's time to fly.
Spread your wings, (*Move in circles with outstretched arms.*)
We're way up high.
Now we're landing in a tree. (*Bend knees and fold arms into body.*)
Here's my sound,
You know it's me.
"Whoo! Whoo!"
What am I? (*Owl*)

Flap your wings, (*Flap arms.*)
It's time to fly.
Spread your wings, (*Move in circles with outstretched arms.*)
We're way up high.
Now we're landing in a tree. (*Bend knees and fold arms into body.*)
Here's my sound,
You know it's me.
"Caw! Caw!"
What am I? (*Crow*)

Flap your wings, (*Flap arms.*)
It's time to fly.
Spread your wings, (*Move in circles with outstretched arms.*)
We're way up high.
Now we're landing in a tree. (*Bend knees and fold arms into body.*)
Here's my sound,
You know it's me.
"Polly wants a cracker!"
What am I? (*Parrot*)

Flap your wings, (*Flap arms.*)
It's time to fly.
Spread your wings, (*Move in circles with outstretched arms.*)
We're way up high.
Back down to a lake instead of a tree.
(*Bend knees and fold arms into body.*)
Here's my sound,
You know it's me.
"Quack! Quack!"
What am I? (*Duck*)

5 Fun Backup Picture Books

Build, Dogs, Build: A Tall Tail by James Horvath. Illustrated by the author. HarperCollins, 2014.

- -

Several construction worker dogs knock down an old building with a crane and wrecking ball. The building falls with a loud "BOOM!" The dogs clean up the site and grab a quick snack from the food truck while "Duke the foreman double-checks the plan." While they are building a new structure, a truck carrying balls crashes. The cry goes out: "Fetch, dogs, fetch!" The crew finally finishes the new building and enjoys the swimming pool on the penthouse terrace.

Falcon by Tim Jessell. Illustrated by the author. Random House, 2012.

- -

For those looking for a non-anthropomorphic animal book, this one features a boy imagining that he's a falcon. The falcon flies in the mountains and over oceans and arrives "to the man-made cliffs of a great booming city." It perches up high on a skyscraper and then plummets downward to startle people. "Oh, if only I were a falcon," says the boy.

Flight School by Lita Judge. Illustrated by the author. Atheneum, 2014.

- -

Penguin wants to learn to fly. He tells the birds at the flight school, "I have the soul of an eagle." One by one, all of the birds at the school succeed at flying, all except Penguin. Flamingo tries to help by attaching several bird feathers to Penguin. Penguin does fly, sort of, with the help of the other birds. His dream has come true and he returns to the flight school with another bird. "My friend Ostrich has the soul of a swallow," he tells the flight instructor.

Let's Have a Tree Party! **by David Martin. Illustrated by John Manders. Candlewick, 2012.**

Grandpa Crow hosts a party in the top of a tree. His guests include "one squirrel and two raccoons, three moths in three cocoons, four possums upside down, and Baby Bear, our favorite clown." The other guests include five frogs, six blue jays, seven ladybugs, eight snakes, nine mice, and ten slugs. They play games such as Follow the Leader and Simon Says. At night, they rest until the nocturnal animals (including owls, bats, and fireflies) arrive to party.

Sally's Great Balloon Adventure **by Stephen Huneck. Illustrated by the author. Abrams, 2010.**

Sally is a dog. Her family takes her to a hot air balloon festival. Sally hops into the basket of an unattended balloon and takes off up into the air. "The people look like little tiny dots far, far below." The news media cover Sally's plight. People think of different ideas to rescue her. Sally finally tugs on the right rope, and the balloon lands safely.

LOST AND FOUND

STORIES AND ACTIVITIES ABOUT BEING LOST AND LOSING AND FINDING THINGS

★ Opening Picture Book: *Otis and the Puppy* by Loren Long

★ Picture Book: *Nini Lost and Found* by Anita Lobel

★ Musical Activity: "My Little Kitten Ran Away" by Rob Reid

★ Picture Book: *Baby Bear* by Kadir Nelson

★ Fingerplay: "The Three Little Kittens Weren't the Only Ones to Lose Things," traditional; adapted by Rob Reid

★ Picture Book: *Found* by Salina Yoon

★ Movement Activity: "Have You Seen My Worm?" by Rob Reid

★ Closing Art Project: Wanted Posters

Opening Picture Book

Otis and the Puppy **by Loren Long. Illustrated by the author. Philomel, 2013.**

The farmer brings a new puppy to the farm. The puppy is afraid of the night and is comforted by Otis, an anthropomorphic tractor. The next day, during a game of hide-and-seek, the puppy wanders off. Night falls, and Otis heads out into the woods to search for the missing puppy. The two eventually make their way back home.

STORYTELLING TIPS: The author adds little italicized sound effects phrases throughout the text, like "putt puff puttedy chuff" and "arrhhr . . . arrhhr . . . arrhf." When you come to each phrase, pause and ask the kids to make those sounds. When Otis is afraid in the woods, slow down your reading to heighten the tension just a tad.

Picture Book

Nini Lost and Found **by Anita Lobel. Illustrated by the author. Knopf, 2010.**

One day, Nini the cat notices that the front door is open. She heads outside. "'I like it,' thought Nini." She walks and walks until she can no longer see her house. "'Oh, this is really, really, really nice,' thought Nini." However, the outdoors becomes scary when it gets dark. Other animals slink around in the nighttime, and a big bird hoots. "'This is not so nice anymore,' thought Nini." She hears her owners calling her name and runs back home. Nini decides that outdoors is nice for a little while, but "home is much, much, much nicer . . . for now."

STORYTELLING TIPS: Nini is inquisitive and reflects her thoughts about her new discoveries with a light tone. When it's nighttime, add a hushed urgency to your voice.

Musical Activity

"My Little Kitten Ran Away" by Rob Reid.

- -

Sing to the tune of the traditional song "Bingo." The melody can be found on the Internet as well as the following children's music recordings: *We All Live Together, Vol. 4* by Greg and Steve (Youngheart, 1980) and *Wee Sing Animals, Animals, Animals* by Pamela Beall and Susan Nipp (Price Stern Sloan, 1999).

My little kitten ran away,
Oh where, oh where is she?
Kitty! Clap, clap, clap! (*Shout "Kitty" with cupped hands and then clap three times in rhythm to the "Bingo" song.*)
Kitty! Clap, clap, clap!
Kitty! Clap, clap, clap!
My kitty's back with me!

My little puppy ran away,
Oh where, oh where is he?
Puppy! Clap, clap, clap! (*Shout "Puppy" with cupped hands and then clap three times in rhythm to the "Bingo" song.*)
Puppy! Clap, clap, clap!
Puppy! Clap, clap, clap!
My puppy's back with me!

Picture Book

Baby Bear by Kadir Nelson. Illustrated by the author. Balzer & Bray, 2014.

- -

Baby Bear is lost and asks several animals for help. Mountain Lion tells Baby Bear to retrace his steps. Frog tells Baby Bear not to be afraid. The squirrels give silly advice— they tell him to hug a tree. Moose finds Baby Bear doing so and advises the cub to listen to his heart. Ram finds Baby Bear crying and suggests he climb a little higher to see all around. "And sing a song—it will make you feel better." Owl hears the song and comforts Baby Bear by saying the little one is not alone. Salmon will show the way home "if you promise not to eat me." As the sun rises, Baby Bear sees that he is home.

> **STORYTELLING TIPS:** This nighttime book should be read with a gentle voice even though Baby Bear is scared. The other animals (except for the squirrels) give comfort and are not fearsome. If you switch voices and play around with their dialogue, do so with moderation.

Fingerplay

"The Three Little Kittens Weren't the Only Ones to Lose Things," traditional; adapted by Rob Reid.

Three little *kittens* lost their *mittens*, (*Hold up three fingers.*)
And they began to cry.
"Meow, meow, meow, meow,"
(*Make meowing sounds while wiggling fists on eyes.*)
"Why, oh why, oh why?"
(*Hold up hands, palms upward, sad expression on face.*)

Three little *ants* lost their *pants*, (*Hold up three fingers.*)
And they began to cry.
"Bibbly-boo, bibbly-boo,"
(*Make antennae with fingers while making these nonsensical sounds.*)
"Why, oh why, oh why?"
(*Hold up hands, palms upward, sad expression on face.*)

Three little *apes* lost their *capes*, (*Hold up three fingers.*)
And they began to cry.
"Ooh-ooh-ooh, ooh-ooh-ooh," (*Scratch head while making the noises.*)
"Why, oh why, oh why?"
(*Hold up hands, palms upward, sad expression on face.*)

Three little *bats* lost their *caps*, (*Hold up three fingers.*)

And they began to cry.

"Flip-flap, flip-flap," (*Make wings out of hands.*)

"Why, oh why, oh why?"

(*Hold up hands, palms upward, sad expression on face.*)

Three little *doves* lost their *gloves*, (*Hold up three fingers.*)

And they began to cry.

"Coo-coo, coo-coo,"

(*Bob head back and forth while crying with fists on eyes.*)

"Why, oh why, oh why?"

(*Hold up hands, palms upward, sad expression on face.*)

Three little *goats* lost their *coats*, (*Hold up three fingers.*)

And they began to cry.

"Baa-baa, baa-baa," (*Make baa-ing sounds while wiggling fists on eyes.*)

"Why, oh why, oh why?"

(*Hold up hands, palms upward, sad expression on face.*)

Three little *llamas* lost their *pajamas*, (*Hold up three fingers.*)

And they began to cry.

"Bleat, bleat, bleat, bleat,"

(*Make bleating sounds while wiggling fists on eyes.*)

"Why, oh why, oh why?"

(*Hold up hands, palms upward, sad expression on face.*)

Three little *flies* lost their *ties*, (*Hold up three fingers.*)

And they began to cry.

"Buzz, buzz, buzz, buzz,"

(*Make buzzing sounds while wiggling fists on eyes.*)

"Why, oh why, oh why?"

(*Hold up hands, palms upward, sad expression on face.*)

They searched and they tossed and they *found* what they lost!

They all made a great big sigh.

Their spirits did shine and they all got in line

And ate a great big piece of pie.

Picture Book

Found by Salina Yoon. Illustrated by the author. Walker, 2014.

- -

A bear finds a toy bunny in the forest. He makes a stack of fliers announcing that the bunny has been found. "But no one came for the bunny." Bear becomes attached to the bunny. They play a lot of games together and have a picnic. One day, a moose calls out, "Floppy, my bunny!" Bear is crushed. Surprisingly, the moose asks Bear to take care of Floppy. "The bunny wasn't lost anymore."

> **STORYTELLING TIPS:** After reading the story, take time to show the kids some of the special lost and found fliers located on the endpapers as well as in the middle of the book. Many will strike a chord with any adults in the audience, such as "LOST MY MARBLES! HELP!," "LOST MY TRAIN OF THOUGHT . . . ," "LOST SHADOW" (with a silhouette of Peter Pan), and "ANYONE SEEN AN ELEPHANT IN THE ROOM?"

Movement Activity

"Have You Seen My Worm?" by Rob Reid.

- -

Have you seen my worm?
I lost my worm.
You'll know it's my worm
'Cause it moves like this . . . (*Move one hand around in a wiggly motion.*)

Have you seen my frog?
I lost my frog.
You'll know it's my frog
'Cause it moves like this . . . (*Jump around the room.*)

Have you seen my fish?
I lost my fish.

You'll know it's my fish
'Cause it moves like this . . . (*Place hands with palms facing backward in front of ears to make fins. Move them, open and shut mouth, and walk around.*)

Have you seen my mole?
I lost my mole.
You'll know it's my mole
'Cause it moves like this . . . (*Hold hands out front as if digging. Blink while moving.*)

Have you seen my hen?
I lost my hen.
You'll know it's my hen
'Cause it moves like this . . . (*Tuck arms into body to make wings; strut around the room.*)

Have you seen my penguin?
I lost my penguin.
You'll know it's my penguin
'Cause it moves like this . . . (*Arms at sides, waddle around the room.*)

Have you seen my elephant?
I lost my elephant.
You'll know it's my elephant
'Cause it moves like this . . . (*Lumber around the room with arm swaying in front of nose to represent a trunk.*)

Add any other animals to stretch out this activity. When you have finished the last animal, stop, point to the kids, and state, "Found it!"

Closing Art Project

Wanted Posters

Before the children leave the program area, give them paper and crayons or markers to create their own "Lost" posters of whatever they want. To help inspire them, display the pages of posters from both the picture book *Found* by Yoon and the backup picture book *Puppy Is Lost* by Ziefert and Woods.

5 Fun Backup Picture Books

I Want My Hat Back by Jon Klassen. Illustrated by the author. Candlewick, 2011.

- -

A bear loses its red hat and wants it back. The bear asks a fox, a frog, a rabbit, a turtle, a snake, and a strange-looking animal that may be a wombat. "Nobody has seen my hat," laments the bear. Suddenly, he sits up and realizes something. "I HAVE SEEN MY HAT." He races past all of the animals and confronts the rabbit, who is wearing a red hat. Afterward, we see the bear wearing his hat and getting a little defensive when a squirrel asks, "Have you seen a rabbit wearing a hat?"

Lost Cat by C. Roger Mader. Illustrated by the author. Houghton Mifflin, 2013.

- -

Slipper the cat lives "with a little old lady in a little old house in a little old town." Life is good for Slipper. When the old lady moves, Slipper is forgotten in the commotion. The cat runs after the moving van but is soon lost in the outdoors. Slipper checks out potential new owners, but there's something lacking about each one. Slipper finally adopts a little girl she names Miss Shiny Shoes.

My Special One and Only by Joe Berger. Illustrated by the author. Dial, 2012.

- -

Bridget takes Captain Cat, her "special one and only" toy cat, to Dingle Bang's Universe of Toys store. Bridget promptly loses Captain

Cat during her shopping spree. She and her friend Billy notice that Captain Cat has fallen into the backpack of another little girl, who is now outside on the sidewalk. Bridget quickly buys another toy cat for the little girl and a button that reads "I GOT LOST IN DINGLE BANG'S."

Puffin Pete by Petr Horáček. Illustrated by the author. Candlewick, 2013.

Two puffins named Peter and Paul were best friends. One day, Peter got lost during a storm. "He was blown far out to sea." He started looking for Paul and sought help from a blue whale. Peter told the whale, "I've lost my best friend, Paul." They go to an island where they find parrots but not Paul. They next find penguins but no Paul. They find a toucan but no Paul. They sadly drift for a few days and come upon some tiny islands. There, they find Paul.

Puppy Is Lost by Harriet Ziefert. Illustrated by Noah Woods. Blue Apple, 2011.

Max looks everywhere for his lost puppy. "Under the bushes . . . behind the trash bins . . . and near the sandbox." Max loses his appetite and has a scary dream in the middle of the night. He makes "Lost Dog" posters and places them all around town. Max decides to head to the last place he saw his puppy just as his lost dog has the same thought. They are reunited. "'Now you're not a lost puppy,' said Max. 'You are found.'"

I'VE GOT A BIG PROBLEM

STORIES AND ACTIVITIES
ABOUT PROBLEM SOLVING

PROGRAM AT A GLANCE

★ Opening Picture Book: *Open Very Carefully: A Book with a Bite* by Nick Bromley and Nicola O'Byrne

★ Picture Book: *Ding Dong! Gorilla!* by Michelle Robinson and Leonie Lord

★ Fingerplay: "Five Little Alligators," traditional; adapted by Rob Reid

★ Picture Book: *That Is NOT a Good Idea!* by Mo Willems

★ Picture Book: *Bandits* by Johanna Wright

★ Movement Activity: "The Raccoon's Hunt," traditional; adapted by Rob Reid

★ Picture Book: *AH HA!* by Jeff Mack

★ Closing Movement / Sound Effects Activity: "AAHH! AAHH!" by Rob Reid

Opening Picture Book

Open Very Carefully: A Book with a Bite by Nick Bromley. Illustrated by Nicola O'Byrne. Nosy Crow, 2013.

The book's narrator tries to read "The Ugly Duckling" but notices a crocodile has snuck into the story. The crocodile starts eating the letters in the book. "I think his favorite letters to eat are O and S." The narrator, accompanied by a duckling, encourages the reader to move the book from side to side to make the crocodile sleepy. The narrator draws a tutu, slippers, and a bow on the sleeping crocodile. Of course, the crocodile wakes up "and he's not looking too happy about that tutu." The crocodile escapes from the book by chewing a hole through the back cover. There is an actual hole.

STORYTELLING TIPS: As you read the voice of the narrator, take long pauses and interact with your audience members at the appropriate times. For example, when the narrator says, "There's something in this book that shouldn't be here," let the kids linger over the picture long enough to spot the crocodile's tail. Let them guess what it is. When you move the book side to side to make the crocodile fall asleep, physically move the book slower and slower until the crocodile nods off. Be sure to do a big double take when everyone discovers the hole in the book.

Picture Book

Ding Dong! Gorilla! by Michelle Robinson. Illustrated by Leonie Lord. Peachtree, 2013.

A boy who ordered a pizza realizes he has a big problem when a gorilla shows up at the door instead of the pizza boy. The gorilla barges past the boy and grabs some crayons. "He did LOTS of COL-ORING, but he wasn't very good at staying between the lines." The gorilla goes on to watch the boy's movies, dress up in different clothes, tear up the garden, and break a vase, a window, and a chair.

When the pizza boy finally arrives, the gorilla grabs all of the pizza and leaves. At least, that's what the boy tells his mother.

STORYTELLING TIPS: The story line is broken up with variations of the repetitive phrase, "That's not the BAD news." When you read those lines, move your eyes toward the floor in a shifty manner to give subtle hints that you're stretching the truth.

Fingerplay

"Five Little Alligators," traditional; adapted by Rob Reid.

This activity is inspired by the traditional fingerplay "Five Little Monkeys." Have the children stand.

Five little gators floating 'neath a tree, (*Hold up five fingers.*)
Teasing Big Gorilla, "You can't catch me!"
(*Put thumbs in ears and wiggle all fingers.*)
Big Gorilla snuck around as quiet as could be,
(*Put pointer finger to lips to signal "be quiet."*)
And grabbed one gator from behind that tree.
(*Make a grabbing motion with one hand.*)

Four little gators floating 'neath a tree, (*Hold up four fingers.*)
Teasing Big Gorilla, "You can't catch me!"
(*Put thumbs in ears and wiggle all fingers.*)
Big Gorilla snuck around as quiet as could be,
(*Put pointer finger to lips to signal "be quiet."*)
And grabbed one gator from behind that tree.
(*Make a grabbing motion with one hand.*)

Three little gators floating 'neath a tree, (*Hold up three fingers.*)
Teasing Big Gorilla, "You can't catch me!"
(*Put thumbs in ears and wiggle all fingers.*)

Big Gorilla snuck around as quiet as could be,
(*Put pointer finger to lips to signal "be quiet."*)
And grabbed one gator from behind that tree.
(*Make a grabbing motion with one hand.*)

Two little gators floating 'neath a tree, (*Hold up two fingers.*)
Teasing Big Gorilla, "You can't catch me!"
(*Put thumbs in ears and wiggle all fingers.*)
Big Gorilla snuck around as quiet as could be,
(*Put pointer finger to lips to signal "be quiet."*)
And grabbed one gator from behind that tree.
(*Make a grabbing motion with one hand.*)

One little gator floating 'neath a tree, (*Hold up one finger.*)
Teasing Big Gorilla, "You can't catch me!"
(*Put thumbs in ears and wiggle all fingers.*)
Big Gorilla snuck around as quiet as could be,
(*Put pointer finger to lips to signal "be quiet."*)
And grabbed that gator from behind that tree.
(*Make a grabbing motion with one hand.*)

No little gators floating 'neath that tree, (*Shake head.*)
No little gators singing, "Can't catch me!" (*Shrug shoulders.*)
Big Gorilla looked around as quiet as could be,
(*Hand over eyes, look around.*)
Then sat right down and rested 'neath that tree.
(*Smile, nod, and sit down.*)

Picture Book

**That Is NOT a Good Idea!* by Mo Willems. Illustrated by the author.
Balzer & Bray, 2013.*

A fox invites a "plump goose" for a stroll. When the goose agrees, the
baby geese warn, "That is NOT a good idea!" The fox insists that he

and the goose head for the woods. The goose says, "Sounds fun!" while the baby geese warn, "That is REALLY NOT a good idea!" This pattern continues as the fox leads the goose to his kitchen where he boils some water. The goose knocks the fox in the water, and the baby geese exclaim, "Well, we DID try to warn him."

STORYTELLING TIPS: Read the variations of the baby geese's lines with increasing energy. The lines build up to the humorous "That is REALLY, REALLY, REALLY, *REALLY* NOT a good idea!" Read the large goose's ongoing lines with wide-eyed innocence and then practically purr out the line that marks the book's turn of events: "Oh—a key ingredient IS missing." Then yell out, "YOU!"

Picture Book

Bandits by Johanna Wright. Illustrated by the author. Roaring Brook, 2011.

Raccoon bandits prowl through the night. "They sneak and they creep. Doing just what they please." That includes stealing laundry from a clothesline and apples from an apple tree and taunting a dog. They run away when spotted by a human family. Back at their lair, "they split up the loot."

STORYTELLING TIPS: Read in a "crime noir" movie voice to capture the tone of the raccoon bandits and their activities.

Movement Activity

"The Raccoon's Hunt," traditional; adapted by Rob Reid.

This activity is based on the traditional activity "Going on a Bear Hunt." It appears in a slightly different form in my book *Welcome to Storytime*. Have the kids slap their legs and repeat each line after you and mime other actions indicated in the dialogue.

Leader: We're going on a hunt for food.
Audience: We're going on a hunt for food.
Leader: We're creeping past a human's house.
Audience: We're creeping past a human's house.
Leader: Ssshhh!
Audience: Ssshhh!
Leader: We need to be quiet.
Audience: We need to be quiet.
Leader: What's that?
Audience: What's that?
Leader: Bark! Bark! Bark! Bark! Bark! Bark!
Audience: Bark! Bark! Bark! Bark! Bark! Bark!
Leader: Oh, no! Look, a dog!
Audience: Oh, no! Look, a dog!
Leader: Run away!
Audience: Run away!
Leader: Whew, that was TOO close.
Audience: Whew, that was TOO close.
Leader: Let's try again, OK?
Audience: Let's try again, OK?

Leader: We're going on a hunt for food.
Audience: We're going on a hunt for food.
Leader: We're creeping past a human's house.
Audience: We're creeping past a human's house.
Leader: Ssshhh!
Audience: Ssshhh!
Leader: We need to be quiet.
Audience: We need to be quiet.
Leader: What's that?
Audience: What's that?
Leader: Honk! Honk! Honk! Honk!

Audience: Honk! Honk! Honk! Honk!

Leader: Oh, no! Look, a car!

Audience: Oh, no! Look, a car!

Leader: Run away!

Audience: Run away!

Leader: Whew, that was TOO close.

Audience: Whew, that was TOO close.

Leader: Let's try again, OK?

Audience: Let's try again, OK?

Leader: We're going on a hunt for food.

Audience: We're going on a hunt for food.

Leader: We're creeping past a human's house.

Audience: We're creeping past a human's house.

Leader: Ssshhh!

Audience: Ssshhh!

Leader: We need to be quiet.

Audience: We need to be quiet.

Leader: What's that?

Audience: What's that?

Leader: Hey, it's a trash can!

Audience: Hey, it's a trash can!

Leader: Oops! Oops! We knocked it over!

Audience: Oops! Oops! We knocked it over!

Leader: Crash! Crash! Rattle! Bang!

Audience: Crash! Crash! Rattle! Bang!

Leader: Oh well.

Audience: Oh well.

Leader: Let's eat!

Audience: Let's eat!

Leader: Please pass the fish heads.

Audience: Please pass the fish heads.

Leader: Yum! Yum! YUM!

Audience: Yum! Yum! YUM!

Picture Book

AH HA! by Jeff Mack. Illustrated by the author. Chronicle, 2013.

- -

This story of a frog chased by a boy, a turtle, an alligator, and a flamingo features only four phrases: "AAHH!," "AH HA!," "AHHH!," and "HA HA!"

STORYTELLING TIPS: This is a wonderful book to interpret phrasing. The presentation will most likely be different every time you read it. It's short enough that a second reading might be in order, with the kids in the audience repeating each line after you.

Closing Movement / Sound Effects Activity

"AAHH! AAHH!" by Rob Reid.

- -

Instruct the children to jump up and down every time the frog jumps. They can also chime in with the frog's lines "AAHH! AAHH! AAHH!" and "HA! HA! HA!"

A boy tried to catch a frog, frog, frog,
He trapped the frog in a bog, bog, bog.
The frightened frog cried: "AAHH! AAHH! AAHH!"
But he JUMPED, got away, and said: "HA! HA! HA!"

A turtle tried to catch a frog, frog, frog,
It trapped the frog in a bog, bog, bog.
The frightened frog cried: "AAHH! AAHH! AAHH!"
But he JUMPED, got away, and said: "HA! HA! HA!"

A gator tried to catch a frog, frog, frog,
It trapped the frog in a bog, bog, bog.
The frightened frog cried: "AAHH! AAHH! AAHH!"
But he JUMPED, got away, and said: "HA! HA! HA!"

A bird tried to catch a frog, frog, frog,
It trapped the frog in a bog, bog, bog.
The frightened frog cried: "AAHH! AAHH! AAHH!"
But he JUMPED, got away, and said: "HA! HA! HA!"

5 Fun Backup Picture Books

**Bully by Laura Vaccaro Seeger. Illustrated by the author.
Roaring Brook, 2013.**

- -

A young bull is told by a bigger bull to "GO AWAY!" The little bull, in turn, is mean to the other animals. It calls the chicken "CHICKEN!" and the turtle "SLOW POKE!" It calls the pig "PIG" and tells a bee to "BUZZ OFF!" A young goat finally calls the bull "BULLY!" not once, but twice before the message sinks into the bull's head. The bull literally flips out and apologizes to the animals.

**The Chicken Problem by Jennifer Oxley. Illustrated by Billy Aronson.
Random House, 2012.**

- -

A girl named Peg and her cat loved to solve problems. They also loved to eat pie. One day, they were having a picnic with a pig when they noticed they had an extra piece of pie left over. Cat went to the chicken coop and plucked out one small chicken to eat the pie. Problem solved . . . or so they thought. Cat forgot to latch the chicken coop and suddenly, "There were one hundred chickens going crazy all over the place! Chickens leaping! Chickens skipping! Chickens hopping! Chickens doing somersaults! Chickens standing on their heads! Chickens standing on each other's heads!" Peg exclaims, "REALLY BIG PROBLEM!"

Oh No, George! **by Chris Haughton. Illustrated by the author.**
Candlewick, 2012.

George the dog has a problem. He spots a delicious cake in the kitchen, but he had made a promise to be a good dog. "What will George do?" George decides to eat the cake. Next, George spots a cat. "'I said I'd be good,' George thinks, 'but I LOVE to play with Cat.'" George chases the cat. George continues to wrestle with his conscience but proceeds to dig in dirt. After making amends, George goes outside and spots some trash. George loves to dig in trash. The book ends with the question, "What will George do? George?"

Silly Goose's Big Story **by Keiko Kasza. Illustrated by the author.**
Putnam, 2012.

Goose entertains his friends with stories about pirates, dinosaurs, and kings. However, when they act out the parts, Goose always gives himself the role of the hero. His friends want to play the hero sometimes. While they are arguing, they are attacked by a wolf. Goose is captured and about to be turned into a hero sandwich. He begins a story about a wolf-eating monster, convincing enough to scare away the wolf.

Wolf Won't Bite! **by Emily Gravett. Illustrated by the author.**
Simon & Schuster, 2012.

Three pigs capture a wild wolf and announce this fact to the world. The pigs showcase the wolf as a circus act. "I can stand him on a stool!" They also dress the wolf up in a bow, ride him like a horse, make him jump through hoops, and saw him in half for a magic trick. The pigs keep reassuring the audience "BUT WOLF WON'T BITE!" When the pigs place their heads in the wolf's jaws, they discover that the wolf might indeed bite.

COOL, COOL WATER

STORIES AND ACTIVITIES ABOUT ANIMALS THAT LIVE IN AND AROUND WATER (AND EVEN BATHE IN IT!)

Opening Picture Book

The Pigeon Needs a Bath! by Mo Willems. Illustrated by the author.
Hyperion, 2014.

- -

The Pigeon insists he doesn't need a bath, even though he is covered with dirt. "I took one last month! I *think* it was last month." The Pigeon gets defensive and states that perhaps *you* need a bath. Flies are attracted to the Pigeon, but even *they* are repelled by his stench. The Pigeon finally hops into a bathtub and then, of course, refuses to get out.

> **STORYTELLING TIPS:** Mo Willems is a master of dialogue so go with the flow and have fun with the Pigeon's diverse inflections. When the Pigeon is in the bathtub, read the page "TEN HOURS LATER" very boldly, pause, and then read the Pigeon's final line: "Can I stay in the tub forever?" in a quiet but cutesy style. After reading the book, point out that two of Willems's other characters make subtle cameo appearances. The man in the beginning is wearing Knuffle Bunny slippers, and there is a shot of the Duckling on one of the images on the back endpapers.

Movement Activity

"Animal Baths" by Rob Reid.

- -

Everyone stands. Ask the children the following questions. Let them act out how they imagine the animals "take a bath." Movement suggestions are provided.

Have you ever seen a cat take a bath?
Show me how a cat takes a bath. (*Lick hands as if they were paws.*)
Have you ever seen a robin take a bath?
Show me how a robin takes a bath.
(*Mime splashing in a birdbath, arms flapping like wings.*)

Have you ever seen an elephant take a bath?

Show me how an elephant takes a bath.

(*Hold arm in front of nose like a trunk. Pretend to spray water out of it.*)

Have you ever seen a dog take a bath?

Show me how a dog takes a bath.

(*Shake hard like a dog shaking off water.*)

Have you ever seen a fish take a bath?

Fish don't take baths! Or do they? (*Slap hand on forehead.*)

Picture Book

Ribbit! by Rodrigo Folgueira. Illustrated by Poly Bernatene. Knopf, 2012.

Several frogs are surprised to find a pink pig sitting on a rock in the middle of their pond. They are more surprised when the pig says "Ribbit!" Soon, several animals hurry to the pond to see the new visitor. They decide to ask the wise old beetle what to do about the pig. When they return with the wise old beetle, the animals find that the pig has left. The wise old beetle surmises that perhaps the pig only wanted to make new friends. The last two pages show the pig sitting on the branches of a tree saying "Tweet!" and "surrounded by new friends," including those same pond animals.

STORYTELLING TIPS: Look astonished yourself when you read the pig's line "Ribbit," as astonished as the pond animals. The kids will laugh at the look on your face. There are many opportunities for playful dialogue, including the frogs' indignation, the mockery of the raccoon and parrot, and the wisdom of the wise old beetle. And, once again, look astonished when the children in the audience notice that the pond animals (the turtle, the weasel, and even the frogs) are sitting on the tree branches with the pig.

Movement Activity

"A Pig in a Pond" by Rob Reid.

- -

Lead the children in standing every time there is a word that begins with the letter *P* and sitting when there is another word beginning with *P*. Say the chant slowly to allow for the constant up-and-down movements.

A *P*ig in a *P*ond,
A *P*ig in a *P*ond,
How *P*reposterous to have
A *P*ig in a *P*ond!
A *P*ython, a *P*ossum, or a *P*uffin *P*erhaps?
A *P*eacock? A *P*enguin? A *P*ronghorn? No chance!
But a *P*ig in a *P*ond,
A *P*ig in a *P*ond,
I'm tickled *P*ink to think
Of a *P*ig in a *P*ond!

Picture Book

***This Is Not My Hat* by Jon Klassen. Illustrated by the author. Candlewick, 2012.**

- -

A tiny fish swimming along informs us that he's just stolen a hat. "I stole it from a big fish. He was asleep when I did it." Despite the tiny fish's belief that the big fish won't notice his hat is gone, the big fish pursues the thief. Although the little fish knows that stealing is

STORYTELLING TIPS: This is a wonderful book in which the pictures contradict the words. When the little fish states that the big fish won't wake up for a long time, we see the big fish is awake. When the little fish states that a crab won't give away his location, we see the crab pointing the way for the big fish. Pause just a bit before turning each page so the children have time to spot these visual contradictions.

wrong, he'll keep the hat just the same. The tiny fish heads for the plants. "Nobody will ever find me." Of course, the big fish finds him.

Picture Book

Fish Had a Wish by Michael Garland. Illustrated by the author. Holiday House, 2012.

- -

A fish wishes it could fly like a bird, nap on a rock like a turtle, "make a big stink" like a skunk, have spots like a bobcat, buzz like a bee, build a dam like a beaver, have pretty wings like a butterfly, and hiss like a snake. When the fish eats a delicious mayfly, it realizes, "It is good to be a fish. I wish to *stay* a fish. Yes! To stay a fish is what I wish."

STORYTELLING TIPS: Because this is a very short book, read it twice. During the second reading, have the children make motions or sounds for the various animals that the fish mentions. For example, they can buzz like the bee and hiss like the snake. They can pretend to chew wood like the beaver and flap their arms like the bird and butterfly. For the skunk, they can simply hold their noses.

Movement Activity

"What Did I See at the Pond?" by Rob Reid.

- -

Everyone stands. Have the children walk on tiptoes as you recite the words. They can then perform the actions of the animals.

As quiet, as quiet, as quiet as I could be,
I went to the pond and what did I see?
I saw lots of wildlife but then—they saw me!
The frogs jumped into the water! (*Jump.*)
The turtles fell into the water! (*Get down on all fours and fall on side.*)

The beaver slapped the water with his tail!

(*Slap the floor behind you and pretend to dive.*)

The fish darted under the surface of the water!

(*Hold palms together, move hands quickly.*)

The ducks flew off the water and into the air! (*Flap arms and stand.*

Move around as if flying and then pause before the next line.)

The pond was empty, as empty as could be.

But I sat very quietly and what did I see?

One by one, the wildlife returned to me.

The frog jumped back on a lily pad! (*Jump.*)

The turtles climbed up on a log!

(*Get down on the floor and mime climbing.*)

The beaver began to chew on a stick!

(*Hold hands up to mouth and make chewing motions.*)

The fish swam slowly once more! (*Palms together, move hands slowly.*)

And the ducks flew back! (*Stand up, "fly" around, and sit.*)

Closing Picture Book / Musical Activity

The Croaky Pokey! by Ethan Long. Illustrated by the author.
Holiday House, 2011.

- -

Several frogs sitting on lily pads decide to "do the Croaky Pokey!" Several of the frogs play musical instruments while the others sing, "Put your right hand in / Put your right hand out / Put your right hand in / And you wave it all about. / Hop the Croaky Pokey / As we chase a fly around / Right in the froggy's mouth!" One frog tries to catch the fly with its tongue but misses. The other frogs continue singing and dancing with their left hand, right foot, left foot, head, backside, and whole self. The frogs (and soon other birds and animals) try to catch the fly with their tongues after each verse, but they keep missing their target. They all trap themselves in a tangle of tongues. In the end, a fish jumps out of the water and snags the fly. "That's what it's all about."

5 Fun Backup Picture Books

I'm a Shark by Bob Shea. Illustrated by the author. Balzer & Bray, 2011.

A shark brags that it is awesome. "When I get a shot, I don't even cry. I can watch scary movies without closing my eyes." However, there is one thing the shark is afraid of. "Creepy spider! Yuck! Is it on me? EWWW! EWWW! EWWW!" The shark goes on to boast that it is not afraid of the dark or bears, just as long as there are no spiders nearby. "Is the big mean bear holding a creepy spider?" The shark finally admits that swimming away from spiders is not being scared, it's being smart.

Mr. Duck Means Business by Tammi Sauer. Illustrated by Jeff Mack. Simon & Schuster, 2011.

Duck lives alone at the pond and posts several Keep Out signs. One day, a pig does a cannonball dive into Duck's pond. "Mr. Duck sputtered. He muttered. He tail-a-fluttered. But Pig did *not* get the message." Duck is about to instruct Pig about private property when, all of a sudden, Cow jumps into the pond. They are joined by all of the farm animals. Duck's peace and quiet is shattered. He finally chases everyone away, but once they are gone, Duck becomes lonely. He decides to post a sign that states "NOISE WELCOME FROM 2:00 PM to 4:00 PM." He is rejoined by his new friends.

Octopus Alone by Divya Srinivasan. Illustrated by the author. Viking, 2013.

Octopus becomes shy when she notices three seahorses staring at her. She tries to shoo them away, but they assume she is playing a game with them. She changes her color, and the seahorses lose sight of her. Octopus goes on with her daily routines, including eluding a hungry eel and dodging a large whale. She also wiggles and twirls and somersaults. After exploring all aspects of the reef, Octopus spots the three seahorses and is "glad to be back with her friends."

One Frozen Lake by Deborah Jo Larson. Illustrated by Steve Johnson and Lou Fancher. Minnesota Historical Society, 2012.

A boy and his grandfather go ice fishing on a frozen lake. "Seven hours pass. Not one fish. Has anyone seen a fish?" The reader spots several fish swimming past the lures just a few inches below the ice. The boy finally lands a "keeper," but the grandfather indicates that they should throw it back. "One frozen lake, good-bye. Two fishing friends, good night. Three miles 'til home. Sweet dreams." Tomorrow, there will be another frozen lake to fish.

Solomon Crocodile by Catherine Rayner. Illustrated by the author. Farrar, Straus and Giroux, 2011.

All of the birds and animals are relaxing by the river when "uh-oh, here comes trouble!" Solomon the crocodile "splats and slops through the mud to make the frogs jump." The frogs tell Solomon to go away. Solomon proceeds to bother the dragonflies and storks. After some hippos chase Solomon away, he feels sad. "Poor Solomon. No one wants to play." At this point, Solomon notices that something is bothering the frogs, dragonflies, and storks. It's another crocodile. "Uh-oh, here comes DOUBLE TROUBLE!"

FOREST FRIENDS

STORIES AND ACTIVITIES
SET IN THE WOODS

★ Opening Picture Book: *Red Hat* by Lita Judge

★ Picture Book: *Bear Has a Story to Tell* by Philip C. Stead and
   Erin E. Stead

★ Musical Activity: "Over in the Forest," traditional; adapted
   by Rob Reid

★ Picture Book / Puppets: *Mario Makes a Move* by Jill McElmurry

★ Fingerplay: "Five Little Squirrels," traditional

★ Picture Book: *Who's in the Forest?* by Phillis Gershator and
   Jill McDonald

★ Closing Imagination Exercise: "I Spy Nature Trail," traditional

Opening Picture Book

Red Hat by Lita Judge. Illustrated by the author. Atheneum, 2013.

A child washes a red hat and leaves it to dry on a clothesline. A bear cub becomes interested and runs off with the hat. A raccoon grabs on to part of the hat with a cry of "Hiii-ya!" Other animals join in as the raccoon runs into the woods. The hat unravels with each step. A mouse and a bunny grab on to one end and go for a wild ride as the baby bear reclaims the hat. The young animals all pull up short with a "Wut-whoa" when a large bear stops what they are doing and points the way back to the child's house. The puzzled child finds that the long strand of yarn is all that remains of the hat and proceeds to knit a new one (as well as a few sweaters for the rabbits).

STORYTELLING TIPS: Sound effects are the sole words in the text. Color each phrase with your voice. Use a high-pitched washing noise when the child cleans the hat: "Swish swash swish swash." I find myself using a Scooby-Doo television character noise with the various bear sounds, such as "Hrmmm?" and "Wut-whoa." Make a martial arts–style, high-pitched "Hiii-ya" for the raccoon and a high-pitched "Yoo-ha" for the mouse. The mouse says "Whoa" twice. The first time this happens, the mouse is in the foreground of the picture. Make that one loud. The next page shows the mouse tucked in the background with a small "Whoa" on the page. Say this one as if you, too, were in the distance.

Picture Book

Bear Has a Story to Tell by Philip C. Stead. Illustrated by Erin E. Stead. Roaring Brook, 2012.

Bear is getting sleepy because winter is approaching. He feels the urge to tell a story before he hibernates. Mouse is too busy to listen. Bear helps Mouse gather seeds for the long winter before Mouse tunnels underground. Duck is too busy to hear Bear's story. Duck has to fly south. Bear checks the wind direction and watches Duck depart. Frog needs to find a warm place to sleep, and Bear digs a proper hole. Frog hops in. Mole is already asleep underground. Bear sees the snowflakes falling and goes to sleep himself. In the spring, Bear is happy he has a chance to tell his story. He greets all of the animals, and they settle down for his story. Unfortunately, Bear cannot remember his story. The friends make suggestions, and Bear begins to tell the story we have just read.

> **STORYTELLING TIPS:** This is a nice, quiet selection. Deliver the story with a slow pace to match the winding down of the characters as they get ready for winter. Add a bit more energy to your vocalization when spring arrives in the story, but not too much.

Musical Activity

"Over in the Forest," traditional; adapted by Rob Reid.

Sing to the tune of the traditional song "Over in the Meadow." The melody can be found on the Internet as well as the following children's music recordings: *Animal Songs* by Susie Tallman (Rock Me Baby Records, 2012) and *Wee Sing Nursery Rhymes and Lullabies* by Pamela Beall and Susan Nipp (Price Stern Sloan, 1985).

Over in the forest
Underneath a tall tree,
Was a mama black bear
And her little cubbies three.
"Growl!" said the mama,
"We'll growl!" said the three,
And they growled and were glad
Underneath that tall tree. (*Everyone growl.*)

Over in the forest
Halfway up a tall tree,
Was a mama woodpecker
And her little fledglings three.
"Hammer!" said the mother,
"We'll hammer!" said the three,
And they hammered and were glad
Halfway up that tall tree.
(*Hammer by touching nose to the palm of your hand back and forth.*)

Over in the forest
Near the top of a tree,
Was a mama flying squirrel
And her little squirrelies three.
"Glide!" said the mama,
"We'll glide!" said the three,
And they glided and were glad
Near the top of the tree.
(*Have the kids stand. Hold arms out and twirl in a circle.*)

Picture Book / Puppets

Mario Makes a Move by Jill McElmurry. Illustrated by the author.
Schwartz & Wade, 2012.

Mario the squirrel likes to make moves such as the "Super Looper"
and the "Rocket to Mars." He also does a not-so-amazing "Flop." His
latest move is to leap from one tree to another. His friend Isabelle says
Mario's move is *nice*. Mario is insulted. He wants her to be *amazed*.
Isabelle shows him her amazing move. Mario accuses her of stealing
his move (the two moves don't look anything alike). Mario turns to
collecting sticks instead of creating new moves. Isabelle chides him
and insists that she likes his move. She meant to say his move was
elegant. They teach each other their respective moves.

STORYTELLING TIPS: There are squirrel puppets for sale on the market. This would be a good story to move the puppet as Mario does his different moves. There is one double-page spread where Mario demonstrates thirteen different moves. Manipulate the puppet to duplicate the moves demonstrated in the book. Mario's signature move is one gigantic arc. Make a sound effect to go along with the move, such as "Boiiing!" You can use the same puppet to demonstrate Isabelle's move or use two puppets, one for each character. If you use two puppets (and have an assistant hold the book), you can demonstrate the last illustration in the book of the two squirrels leaping together and grabbing hands.

Fingerplay

"Five Little Squirrels," traditional.

- -

Five little squirrels with acorns to store. (*Hold up five fingers.*)
One went to sleep and then there were four!
(*Mime sleeping with head on hands and then hold up four fingers.*)
Four little squirrels hunting acorns in a tree. (*Mime climbing a tree.*)
One fell down, and now there are three! (*Hold up three fingers.*)
Three little squirrels wondering what to do. (*Shrug shoulders.*)
One got lost, and now there are two! (*Hold up two fingers.*)
Two little squirrels tossing acorns for fun. (*Mime playing catch.*)
One got tired, and now there is one! (*Hold up one finger.*)
One little squirrel playing in the sun.
(*Look up at the "sun" with hands over eyes.*)
He ran away, now there are none.
(*Hold up hand with all fingers curled in fist.*)

Picture Book

Who's in the Forest? by Phillis Gershator. Illustrated by Jill McDonald. Barefoot Books, 2010.

- -

The refrain "Who's in the forest, dark and deep?" takes us to birds in the treetops, squirrels gathering acorns, foxes creeping along, bear cubs playing, and owls sleeping. When the sun goes down, the narrator tells us to look at "who's stirring in the forest at night!"

> **STORYTELLING TIPS:** There are die-cut holes in this board book. Even though it's designed as a toddler book, slightly older kids will get excited to see the reveal with each turn of the page.

Closing Imagination Exercise

"I Spy Nature Trail," traditional.

- -

Everyone stands. Using the traditional game that goes "I spy with my little eye," give hints on woodland animals you're pretending to see as you walk around the program area—for example, "I spy with my little eye . . . something big and black eating berries" (a bear) or "I spy with my little eye . . . something with a bushy tail eating nuts" (a squirrel). You don't need to limit your choices to animals: "I spy with my little eye . . . a colorful arc in the sky" (a rainbow). If you are in a public library, you can end the program by saying, "I spy with my little eye . . . big people waiting for you!" (parents and other caregivers).

5 Fun Backup Picture Books

Bear's Loose Tooth by Karma Wilson. Illustrated by Jane Chapman. Margaret K. McElderry, 2011.

- -

Bear and his forest friends were eating lunch when Bear's tooth moved. The birds and animals told Bear to open his mouth wide. They "looked inside and saw Bear's loose tooth." Wren tried to pull the tooth out. "But it stayed stuck tight." Owl tries next. No luck. They all try, but the tooth won't budge. It finally falls out when Bear gives it a little nudge with his tongue. That night, the tooth fairy takes the tooth and leaves a plate of blueberries.

***Cheer Up, Mouse!* by Jed Henry. Illustrated by the author. Houghton Mifflin, 2012.**

- -

Several woodland animals and birds try to make Mouse smile. They grab him and fly him in the air. "Flap and flutter, dip and dive—Cheer up, Mouse! Dizzy heights are for birds. I can wash those tears away." They plunk him in a pond, bounce him on a picnic blanket, put him in a tunnel, and feed him grubs as well. Chipmunk approaches Mouse and gives him a hug. Mouse finally cheers up.

***Children Make Terrible Pets* by Peter Brown. Illustrated by the author. Little, Brown, 2010.**

- -

A bear child named Lucy finds a human boy lost in the woods. She decides to keep him. "OH! MY! GOSH! You are the cutest critter in the WHOLE forest!" yells Lucy. The boy simply squeaks (at least to Lucy's ears), so Lucy names him Squeaker. Her mother warns her that "children make terrible pets." Lucy and Squeaker play together, but he ruins the furniture and refuses to become potty trained. Squeaker finally makes it back to his own human family. Lucy agrees with her mother that "children DO make terrible pets."

***Deer Dancer* by Mary Lyn Ray. Illustrated by Lauren Stringer. Simon & Schuster, 2014.**

- -

A girl dances in a special clearing near the woods. A deer shows up and then runs back "toward the trees where shadows start and woods begin." The girl is inspired by her encounter with the deer. When she practices outdoors another day, the deer returns. The girl dances while the deer grazes. Then the deer "lifts his ears, his nose, his neck—and leaps and turns around me." The deer once more runs into the woods, but the girl continues her deer dance.

Mr. Prickles: A Quill Fated Love Story by Kara LaReau. Illustrated by Scott Magoon. Roaring Brook, 2012.

Mr. Prickles the porcupine has trouble making friends. "By their very nature, porcupines are very hard to get close to." He tried playing with the other nocturnal animals, "but it was pointless." Mr. Prickles becomes prickly on the inside as well as the outside. One night, Mr. Prickles meets another porcupine—Miss Pointypants. They become friends, and Mr. Prickles decides he's no longer prickly on the inside.

ANIMAL BUDDIES

STORIES AND ACTIVITIES
ABOUT UNLIKELY FRIENDS

- ★ Opening Picture Book: *Caterina and the Perfect Party* by Erin Eitter Kono

- ★ Picture Book: *You Will Be My Friend!* by Peter Brown

- ★ Movement Activity: "My Best Friend" by Rob Reid

- ★ Picture Book: *City Dog, Country Frog* by Mo Willems and Jon J. Muth

- ★ Guessing Rhyme: "Guess My Friend" by Rob Reid

- ★ Picture Book: *Good News, Bad News* by Jeff Mack

- ★ Movement Activity: "Alligator Is My Friend," traditional; adapted by Rob Reid

- ★ Closing Picture Book: *Duck, Duck, Moose!* by Sudipta Bardhan-Quallen and Noah Z. Jones

Opening Picture Book

Caterina and the Perfect Party by Erin Eitter Kono. Illustrated by the author.
Dial, 2013.

- -

A brown bird named Caterina is planning her first party. Her decorations are "decorative." Her appetizers are "appetizing." Her wonderful outdoor party is all set, but something goes wrong. It rains, and the wind blows everything around. "Poor Caterina. This is not what she had planned." Fortunately, her friends all show up with treats, musical instruments, decorations, and more. "Her party is the best party anyone has ever seen."

STORYTELLING TIPS: The author does a nice job setting up the pacing of the narrative and matching it with her page layout. Vocalize those little built-in pauses. "The invitations will be . . ." (turn the page) "inviting." The author also wrote several words in bold style for vocal emphasis: "But on the big day, things *do* go wrong. *Really* wrong."

Picture Book

You Will Be My Friend! by Peter Brown. Illustrated by the author.
Little, Brown, 2011.

- -

Lucy the bear wakes up one day and decides to make a new friend. "'The forest is crawling with fun critters. Surely, ONE of them will want to be my friend. This is going to be GREAT!'" Things don't work out well for Lucy as she tries to befriend frogs, a giraffe, a skunk, an ostrich, and several other animals. "Lucy was starting to

STORYTELLING TIPS: For some reason, whenever I read Peter Brown's books about Lucy, I channel Miss Piggy from the Muppets and use her voice for Lucy's dialogue. I'm just saying . . .

feel ridiculous." When everything appears to be hopeless, a flamingo approaches Lucy and the two become friends.

Movement Activity

"My Best Friend" by Rob Reid.

My best friend is Snake!
Here are two things we can do:
We can slide on the grass, (*Get down on bellies.*)
And stick out our tongues, (*Stick tongues in and out quickly.*)
That's what best friends do. (*Back up to sitting position.*)

My best friend is a Monkey!
Here are two things we can do:
We can scratch ourselves, (*Scratch all over.*)
And go "ooh-ooh-ooh," (*Make monkey noises.*)
That's what best friends do.

My best friend is a Beaver!
Here are two things we can do:
We can chew on wood, (*Make chewing motions.*)
And slap our tails, (*Slap hand on floor behind you.*)
That's what best friends do.

My best friend is a Woodpecker!
Here are two things we can do:
We can hammer at trees, (*Move head back and forth.*)
And fly in the sky, (*Flap arms.*)
That's what best friends do.

My best friend is a Hippo!
Here are two things we can do:
We can float real low,
(*Squat down with your eyes peering over your hands.*)

And open our mouths wide, (*Open mouths wide.*)
That's what best friends do.

My best friend is a Sloth!
Here are two things we can do:
We can hang upside-down,
(*Lie down on back with arms in the air, as if hanging from a branch.*)
And move real ss-1l-ooooo-www, (*Stand up slowly.*)
That's what best friends do. (*Applaud.*)

Picture Book

City Dog, Country Frog by Mo Willems. Illustrated by Jon J. Muth.
Hyperion, 2010.

- -

A dog ran into the country and met a frog. The frog explained
that it was waiting for a friend, "but *you'll* do." They had fun playing together in the spring, the summer, and the fall. When winter
arrived, City Dog headed for Country Frog's rock, but "Country Frog
was not there." When spring came back, Country Chipmunk spotted
City Dog sitting on Country Frog's rock. City Dog told the chipmunk
that he was waiting for a friend. "Then he smiled a froggy smile and
said . . . 'But *you'll* do.'"

STORYTELLING TIPS: This is a nice, quiet story with short
episodes marked by the different seasons. Pause after the repetitive
variations about the seasons, such as "That was winter," before moving on.

Guessing Rhyme

"Guess My Friend" by Rob Reid.

- -

Tell the children you made some new friends recently, but they aren't human.
The kids have to guess what they are from the clues in the rhyme. Pause in

the last line of each stanza and let the children guess and fill in the italicized animal word. Afterward, make up your own verses.

> I have a friend, his name is Mark,
> My friend Mark, he likes to bark.
> I have a friend, his name is Mark,
> Mark is a *dog* who likes to bark.

> I have a friend, her name is Patches,
> My friend Patches purrs and scratches.
> I have a friend, her name is Patches,
> Patches is a *cat* who purrs and scratches.

> I have a friend, her name is Michelle,
> My friend Michelle sometimes hides in her shell.
> I have a friend, her name is Michelle,
> Michelle is a *turtle* who sometimes hides in her shell.

> I have a friend, his name is Paul.
> My friend Paul is really, really, REALLY tall.
> I have a friend, his name is Paul,
> Paul is a *giraffe* who is really, really, REALLY tall.

Picture Book

**Good News, Bad News by Jeff Mack. Illustrated by the author.
Chronicle, 2012.**

This short picture book features the two lines "Good news" and "Bad news" over and over as we follow two friends, Rabbit and Mouse. Rabbit holds up a picnic basket. "Good news!" We turn the page and see that it's starting to rain. "Bad news." Rabbit pulls out an umbrella. "Good news." The wind pulls the umbrella (and Mouse) away. "Bad news." This pattern continues until the two friends finally have their picnic.

Movement Activity

"Alligator Is My Friend," traditional; adapted by Rob Reid.

- -

This call-and-response song about an alligator is popular at camp settings. I added verses for elephant and moose. Think of your own verses to add. Ask the children to repeat each line after you.

Leader: The alligator is my friend.
Audience: The alligator is my friend.
Leader: And he can be yours, too.
Audience: And he can be yours, too.
Leader: If only you would understand,
Audience: If only you would understand,
Leader: That he has feelings, too.
Audience: That he has feelings, too.
Leader (*quietly*): Al-li-ga-tor.
(*With both hands, make a small alligator mouth open and shut.*)
Audience (*quietly*): Al-li-ga-tor. (*Audience imitates motions.*)
Leader (*slightly louder*): Al-li-ga-tor!
(*Make larger alligator mouth open and shut.*)
Audience (*slightly louder*): Al-li-ga-tor! (*Audience imitates motions.*)
Leader (*yelling*): AL-LI-GA-TOR!
(*Make overly large alligator mouth open and shut.*)
Audience (*yelling*): AL-LI-GA-TOR! (*Audience imitates motions.*)
Leader (*yelling*): THE ALLIGATOR IS MY FRIEND!
Audience (*yelling*): THE ALLIGATOR IS MY FRIEND!
Leader (*yelling*): AND HE HAS FEELINGS, TOO!
Audience (*yelling*): AND HE HAS FEELINGS, TOO!

Leader: The elephant is my friend.

Audience: The elephant is my friend.

Leader: And he can be yours, too.

Audience: And he can be yours, too.

Leader: If only you would understand,

Audience: If only you would understand,

Leader: That he has feelings, too.

Audience: That he has feelings, too.

Leader (*quietly*): El-e-phant. (*Hold your arm in front of your nose like a trunk. Lift your arm a little bit in the air.*)

Audience (*quietly*): El-e-phant. (*Audience imitates motions.*)

Leader (*slightly louder*): El-e-phant! (*Lift your arm slightly higher.*)

Audience (*slightly louder*): El-e-phant! (*Audience imitates motions.*)

Leader (*yelling*): EL-E-PHANT! (*Lift your arm high in the air.*)

Audience (*yelling*): EL-E-PHANT! (*Audience imitates motions.*)

Leader (*yelling*): THE ELEPHANT IS MY FRIEND!

Audience (*yelling*): THE ELEPHANT IS MY FRIEND!

Leader (*yelling*): AND HE HAS FEELINGS, TOO!

Audience (*yelling*): AND HE HAS FEELINGS, TOO!

Leader: The great-big-moose is my friend.

Audience: The great-big-moose is my friend.

Leader: And he can be yours, too.

Audience: And he can be yours, too.

Leader: If only you would understand,

Audience: If only you would understand,

Leader: That he has feelings, too.

Audience: That he has feelings, too.

Leader (*quietly*): Great-big-moose.

(*Make antlers out of hands and place on both sides of head.*)

Audience (*quietly*): Great-big-moose. (*Audience imitates motions.*)

Leader (*slightly louder*): Great-big-moose!

(*Hold out "antlers" a few inches from head.*)

Audience (*slightly louder*): Great-big-moose! (*Audience imitates motions.*)

Leader (*yelling*): GREAT-BIG-MOOSE! (*Hold "antlers" far from head.*)

Audience (*yelling*): GREAT-BIG-MOOSE! (*Audience imitates motions.*)

Leader (*yelling*): THE GREAT-BIG-MOOSE IS MY FRIEND!

Audience (*yelling*): THE GREAT-BIG-MOOSE IS MY FRIEND!

Leader (*yelling*): AND HE HAS FEELINGS, TOO!

Audience (*yelling*): AND HE HAS FEELINGS, TOO!

Closing Picture Book

Duck, Duck, Moose! by Sudipta Bardhan-Quallen.
Illustrated by Noah Z. Jones. Hyperion, 2014.

- -

Two ducks clean their house, but their friend Moose crashes through the wall and makes a mess. The ducks paint a picture, but Moose clumsily knocks over the paints and easel. The ducks bake a cake, but Moose accidentally smashes it. The ducks throw a surprise party for Moose, but he doesn't show up. The friends all get together once more and, of course, Moose makes a mess.

> **STORYTELLING TIPS:** This is another short picture book with repetitive text that you can read and then turn over the reading chores to your young audience. Point to the ducks and the kids will chant, "Duck, duck, duck, duck . . .," and then point to the moose to cue them when to yell, "Moose!"

5 Fun Backup Picture Books

Everyone Needs a Friend by Dubravka Kolanovic. Illustrated by the author. Price Stern Sloan, 2010.

- -

Jack the wolf keeps busy all year long but is lonely. A lost mouse named Walter wanders by. Jack takes care of Walter, and the two have fun together. "Jack had forgotten how much fun it could be to play with a friend!" Unfortunately, Walter snores and puts Jack in a bad mood. When Walter makes a mess with breakfast, Jack asks him to leave. Jack feels remorse and runs after Walter. Jack learns "that no matter how big a mess Walter made, it was worth it to have his friend around!"

Friends by Michael Foreman. Illustrated by the author. Andersen, 2012.

- -

Cat feels lucky to be able to "wander wild and free, far and wide." He feels sorry for his friend Bubbles. "He's a fish . . . Stuck in his tank." Cat convinces Bubbles to jump into a bucket of water, and he carries his little friend to a pond. He next takes Bubbles to look at a river and then the ocean. "His eyes grew even bigger. He had never seen so much water!" Cat encourages Bubbles to jump into the sea, but Bubbles shakes his head. "There may be lots of other fish in the sea, but I might never find a friend like you." The two continue to wander around looking at the world.

Grumpy Goat by Brett Helquist. Illustrated by the author. HarperCollins, 2013.

- -

Goat arrives at Sunny Acres farm. "Goat had never had a single friend in his life. He didn't want one now." The other farm animals tried to become his friends, but "Goat chased them off." One day, Goat notices a dandelion growing on Sunrise Hill. He takes care of the little plant and is heartbroken when the seeds blow away in the wind. The other animals try to cheer him up, and Goat slowly comes around. His life brightens when the whole hillside becomes covered with dandelions. "All summer long, Goat was happy to be at Sunny Acres . . . once again the friendliest little farm in the county."

Kate & Pippin: An Unlikely Love Story by Martin Springett. Photographs by Isobel Springett. Holt, 2012.

- -

A human family found an abandoned fawn and brought it to their home. A Great Dane named Kate befriended the fawn. "Kate gave the young deer a nuzzle and a lick." The fawn snuggled close to the dog, who felt "being a mom to the little deer came naturally." Kate's owner Isobel named the fawn Pippin. One day, the fawn left the yard. "Kate and Isobel worried they might never see Pippin again." Pippin returned the next morning but slept every night in the woods. Even when she became fully grown, "Pippin always came back to the farm to play with Kate."

Penguin and Pinecone: A Friendship Story by Salina Yoon. Illustrated by the author. Walker, 2012.

One day, Penguin spotted a pinecone in the snow but was not sure what it was. "It was too brown to be a snowball . . . too hard to be food . . . and too prickly to be an egg." Penguin decided the object would be his friend. He took the pinecone to a forest where it was warmer. Much later, Penguin wondered what happened to his friend. He made the trip back to the forest and learned that the pinecone had turned into a tall tree. Even though the forest was too warm for Penguin to stay long, "they always stayed in each other's hearts."

WEIRD AND WONDERFUL PETS
STORIES AND ACTIVITIES ABOUT PETS

★ Opening Picture Book: *A Pet for Petunia* by Paul Schmid

★ Poem: "Skunk" from *The Pet Project: Cute and Cuddly Vicious Verses* by Lisa Wheeler and Zachariah Ohora

★ Song: "Old McDonald Had a Pet Shop," traditional; adapted by Rob Reid

★ Picture Book / Felt Story: *Boot & Shoe* by Marla Frazee

★ Musical Activity: "Dogs and Cats and Guinea Pigs," traditional; adapted by Rob Reid

★ Picture Book: *Some Cat!* by Mary Casanova and Ard Hoyt

★ Picture Book / Creative Dramatics: *How to Be a Cat* by Nikki McClure

★ Poem: "Pet Rock" from *The Pet Project: Cute and Cuddly Vicious Verses* by Lisa Wheeler and Zachariah Ohora

★ Closing Song: "I Know an Old Lady Who Had a Pet Fly," traditional; adapted by Rob Reid

Opening Picture Book

A Pet for Petunia by Paul Schmid. Illustrated by the author.
HarperCollins, 2011.

A little girl named Petunia loves everything about skunks. She has a stuffed animal skunk, but she "wants, wants, wants! a REAL pet skunk." She promises her parents that she'll feed the skunk every day, take it for walks, read it stories, and even clean out its litter box. Petunia becomes very upset when her parents tell her that skunks stink. When Petunia encounters an actual skunk in the woods, she realizes . . . her parents were right. "Petunia smells the worst smell she has ever smelled in her entire life . . . An *awful* stink! A *horrible* stink! A *humongous* stink!" She decides she's happy with her stuffed animal skunk, until she spots an "absolutely, totally, major sweet porcupine!"

STORYTELLING TIPS: When Petunia pleads with her parents, play up her excitement at the thought of a pet skunk. "'Pleeeease?' she begs her parents." Have fun with Petunia's tantrum when she is told skunks stink. "'This is so not fair! I'll tell you what stinks! THIS stinks! You just don't love me. That's what it is. *They* do NOT stink! Stink, my foot! You wanna see stink? I'll show you stink!'"

Poem

"Skunk" from *The Pet Project: Cute and Cuddly Vicious Verses* by Lisa Wheeler.
Illustrated by Zachariah Ohora. Atheneum, 2013.

This four-line poem tells of a she-skunk in search of a he-skunk. The narrator states that despite what the he-skunk thinks, "I think the she-skunk truly stinks."

Song

"Old McDonald Had a Pet Shop," traditional; adapted by Rob Reid.

- -

Sing to the tune of the traditional song, "Old MacDonald." The melody can be found on the Internet as well as the following children's music recordings: *Animal Songs* by Susie Tallman (Rock Me Baby Records, 2012) and *Wee Sing Animals, Animals, Animals* by Pamela Beall and Susan Nipp (Price Stern Sloan, 1999). Instruct the children to make the animal sounds as well as chime in with "E-I-E-I-O."

> Old McDonald had a pet shop, E-I-E-I-O,
> And in this shop he had a dog, E-I-E-I-O,
> With a "woof-woof" here, and a "woof-woof" there,
> Here a "woof," there a "woof," everywhere a "woof-woof,"
> Old McDonald had a pet shop, E-I-E-I-O.

> Old McDonald had a pet shop, E-I-E-I-O,
> And in this shop he had a cat, E-I-E-I-O,
> With a "meow-meow" here, and a "meow-meow" there,
> Here a "meow," there a "meow," everywhere a "meow-meow,"
> Old McDonald had a pet shop, E-I-E-I-O.

> Old McDonald had a pet shop, E-I-E-I-O,
> And in this shop he had a snake, E-I-E-I-O,
> With a "hiss-hiss" here, and a "hiss-hiss" there,
> Here a "hiss," there a "hiss," everywhere a "hiss-hiss,"
> Old McDonald had a pet shop, E-I-E-I-O.

> Old McDonald had a pet shop, E-I-E-I-O,
> And in this shop he had a mouse, E-I-E-I-O,
> With a "squeak-squeak" here, and a "squeak-squeak" there,
> Here a "squeak," there a "squeak," everywhere a "squeak-squeak,"
> Old McDonald had a pet shop, E-I-E-I-O.

Old McDonald had a pet shop, E-I-E-I-O,
And in this shop he had a parrot, E-I-E-I-O,
With a "Polly wants a cracker" here, and a "Polly wants a cracker" there,
Here a "Polly," there a "cracker," everywhere a "Polly wants a cracker,"
Old McDonald had a pet shop, E-I-E-I-O.

Picture Book / Felt Story

Boot & Shoe by Marla Frazee. Illustrated by the author. Beach Lane, 2012.

Boot and Shoe are two dogs that eat together, sleep together, and even "pee on the same tree" together. But Boot is "a back porch kind of dog" and Shoe is "a front porch kind of dog." They spend their days on opposite ends of the house. A squirrel bothers the dogs and "gets all up in their business." The dogs find themselves on opposite ends of the house. They each decide to wait for the other to return to their respective porches. They worry when the other doesn't show up. They walk around the house on opposite ends. "But no luck again." Neither one sleeps well. When daylight arrives, they drag themselves to the tree to pee and are "overjoyed to see each other!" They both head for bed—"Together! (Of course.)"

> **STORYTELLING TIPS:** Make a felt house and two felt dogs. Move the dog pieces at the appropriate ends of the felt house while reading to help audience members visualize the story's setting and the characters placement throughout. The use of a felt squirrel is entirely optional, but the manipulations work well without one.

Musical Activity

"Dogs and Cats and Guinea Pigs," traditional; adapted by Rob Reid.

Sing to the tune of the traditional song "Head Shoulders Knees and Toes." The melody can be found on the Internet as well as the following children's music recordings: *Monkey Sing, Monkey Do* by Mary Lambert (Mary Lambert, 2008) and *Rockin' the Schoolhouse, Vol. 1* by Billy Gorilla (Flying Kitten, 2009). This activity first appeared in my book *Storytime Slam!* Teach the children the following actions to accompany the words:

Dogs: Pant with tongues out.
Cats: Lick back of hand.
Guinea Pigs: Blink as if just waking up and looking around.
Birds: Flap arms as wings.
Fish: Purse lips and hold hands behind ears as if they were gills.
Snakes: Flick tongues in and out.
Mice: Brush behind ears as if cleaning them with paws.

Dogs and cats and guinea pigs,
Guinea pigs.
Dogs and cats and guinea pigs,
Guinea pigs.
Birds and fish and snakes and mice,
Dogs and cats and guinea pigs,
Guinea pigs.

Picture Book

Some Cat! by Mary Casanova. Illustrated by Ard Hoyt.
Farrar, Straus and Giroux, 2012.

Violet the cat is upset that she's in an animal shelter. She hisses at the people who approach her. One day, a couple adopts Violet and takes her home. She hisses at the couple's two dogs, Zippity and George. Three stray dogs chase Violet one afternoon, and they don't back away when she hisses at them. The couple and their dogs chase the stray dogs away "tails down." From that day on, Violet gets along with the other members of her family.

> **STORYTELLING TIPS:** Before you read the book, teach the kids to make hissing noises whenever Violet goes "Meowwww! Hissss! Spat!" The kids can practice and arch their backs and hold up their "claws" while making the noises. They can also make yipping noises when Zippity goes "Ya-yippity, yappity, yee-yee-yeep!" and howl when George goes "Wa-roooo! Wa-roo-roo-roo-roo!" Have everyone purr along with Violet at the end of the story.

Picture Book / Creative Dramatics

How to Be a Cat by Nikki McClure. Illustrated by the author. Abrams, 2013.

A kitten learns important lessons from an older cat. These include stretching, cleaning, pouncing, being brave, listening, exploring, hunting, tumbling, licking, stalking, chasing, waiting, finding, scratching, feasting, and dreaming.

> **STORYTELLING TIPS:** Have the children stand and act out each action as you read it. There are no wrong movements; the kids can act out the actions with whatever creative inspiration comes to mind. Give them about ten seconds to act out each action before moving on to the next one.

Poem

"Pet Rock" from *The Pet Project: Cute and Cuddly Vicious Verses* by Lisa Wheeler. Illustrated by Zachariah Ohora. Atheneum, 2013.

A girl's father remembers once having a pet rock, so the girl gives him a pet boulder as a Father's Day present. At the end of the poem, pull out a rock and show it to the kids. Tell them this is the library's pet and give it a name. Or have a naming contest. The kids can visit and check up on the rock for weeks after the story program.

Closing Song

"I Know an Old Lady Who Had a Pet Fly," traditional; adapted by Rob Reid.

- -

Tell the children that you are going to share a song about someone who has normal pets, like a cat and a dog, but also has weird pets. Sing or read the text to the traditional song "I Know an Old Lady Who Swallowed a Fly." The melody can be found on the Internet as well as the following children's music recordings: *Travel Song Sing-Alongs* by Kevin Roth (Marlboro, 1994) and *Peter, Paul and Mommy Too* by Peter, Paul, and Mary (Warner Brothers, 1993). Feel free to add or swap new verses, particularly if you use picture books that include different pets.

I know an old lady who had a pet fly.
I don't know why she had a pet fly.
I wonder why.

I know an old lady who had a pet spider
That wiggled and jiggled and tickled around her.
She had a pet spider to play with the fly.
I don't know why she had a pet fly.
I wonder why.

I know an old lady who had a pet cat.
Imagine that, she had a pet cat.
She had a pet cat to play with the spider
That wiggled and jiggled and tickled around her.
She had a pet spider to play with the fly.
I don't know why she had a pet fly.
I wonder why.

I know an old lady who had a pet dog.
She went for a jog with her little pet dog.
She had a pet dog to play with the cat.
She had a pet cat to play with the spider
That wiggled and jiggled and tickled around her.

She had a pet spider to play with the fly.
I don't know why she had a pet fly.
I wonder why.

I know an old lady who had a pet skunk.
Who'd have thunk that she had a pet skunk?
She had a pet skunk that went Spritz! Splash! Splat!
That's the end of that.
(*Spoken*) And that's the end of today's story program!

5 Fun Backup Picture Books

Gilbert Goldfish Wants a Pet by Kelly DiPucchio. Illustrated by Bob Shea.
Dial, 2011.

- -

A goldfish decides it wants a pet. It considers "a barky-bark" dog, a
mouse that made Gilbert's heart go "pitter-patter-swish," and a buzzing fly that unfortunately gets swatted. We notice the silhouette of a
cat approaching Gilbert's bowl. The cat turns out to be a catfish that
now lives with Gilbert in the bowl. Gilbert names his new pet Fluffy.

My Snake Blake by Randy Siegel. Illustrated by Serge Bloch.
Roaring Brook, 2012.

- -

A boy's parents give him a "super-long, bright green snake" for his
birthday, even though Mom says, "'I think your father is nuts.'"
The snake twists its body to spell words, including its name, Blake.
Blake wins Mother over with its many talents, including cooking,
catching flies, finding missing car keys, and helping the boy with his
homework.

The Pets You Get! by Thomas Taylor. Illustrated by Adrian Reynolds. Andersen, 2013.

A boy mocks his sister's pet guinea pig as being too boring. He'd rather have a "cool" pet, like a dog or a brown bear or a "huge smoking dragon." The boy slowly changes his mind when he helps his sister chase the guinea pig. He says, "'And he's really hard to catch! What a fantastic game of hide-and-seek!'"

Prudence Wants a Pet by Cathleen Daly. Illustrated by Stephen Michael King. Roaring Brook, 2011.

Prudence's parents won't give her a real pet, so she makes one out of a branch. She names it Branch. Branch breaks and becomes Prudence's new pet, Twig. Prudence goes on to make pets out of a shoe (she puts it on a leash and "takes him for a walk around the block"), her baby brother Milo, a car tire named Mr. Round, and sea buddies. Her parents decide that Prudence should have a pet after all. They get her a dog (or is it a cat?) that she names Branch.

Scooter in the Outside by Anne Bowen. Illustrated by Abby Carter. Holiday House, 2012.

Lucy takes her pet dog Scooter on a daily walk around the block. Scooter wants to veer off the normal route, but Lucy hangs on tight to the leash. One day, Scooter notices the front door has been left open, and he heads outside. He crosses the street but becomes frightened by noisy vehicles: "WEEEEE-OOOOOO-WEEEEE-OOOOO!" Lucy finds him and takes him home.

THE ANIMAL
ELEMENTARY SCHOOL
STORIES AND ACTIVITIES ABOUT SCHOOL

PROGRAM AT A GLANCE

- ★ Opening Picture Book: *Oliver and His Alligator* by Paul Schmid
- ★ Chant/Prop: "Bring a Friend to School" by Rob Reid
- ★ Picture Book: *Rufus Goes to School* by Kim T. Griswell and Valeri Gorbachev
- ★ Movement Activity: "If Pigs Went to Pig School" by Rob Reid
- ★ Picture Book: *Flip & Fin: We Rule the School!* by Timothy Gill and Neil Numberman
- ★ Fingerplay: "Five Little Fish Heading to School" by Rob Reid
- ★ Picture Book: *Is Your Buffalo Ready for Kindergarten?* by Audrey Vernick and Daniel Jennewein
- ★ Closing Movement Activity: "Great Big Buffalo," traditional

Opening Picture Book

Oliver and His Alligator by Paul Schmid. Illustrated by the author.
Hyperion, 2013.

A human child named Oliver is nervous about the first day of school. "Oliver thought it best to stop by the swamp and pick up an alligator. Just in case things got rough." Oliver is intimidated right away when the "lady who wasn't his mom said, 'Welcome to your new school! What might your name be?'" Oliver replies, "'Munch, munch!'" and his alligator swallows the lady. The alligator proceeds to swallow the other kids, and everything becomes quiet. "Then Oliver heard singing. And laughing. And fun!" The sounds were coming from inside the alligator. Oliver gives one last "'Munch, munch!'" and joins the fun.

> **STORYTELLING TIPS:** You can have the children in the audience repeat "Munch, munch" after you read those lines. It happens four times in the book—one time with a whisper voice and the final time with a loud voice. The children might even want to make alligator jaws with their arms. At the very end, ask the kids where the alligator went. Some of them might see the color and shape of the alligator in the round rug at the end. Show them the back endpaper with the alligator in bed and even the alligator in the front endpapers to let them know that it is a toy.

Chant/Prop

"Bring a Friend to School" by Rob Reid.

This activity can be done with stuffed animals as props to connect it to the Paul Schmid book, or it can be done with just simple actions.

Bring a friend to school,
Bring a friend to school, clap, clap. (*Clap twice.*)
Bring a friend to school,
Bring a friend to school, clap, clap. (*Clap twice.*)

I brought a little friend,
My friend is a bunny. (*Hold up a toy bunny and let the kids shout out what it is or make bunny ears behind your head.*)
Bring a friend to school,
Bring a friend to school, clap, clap. (*Clap twice.*)
Bring a friend to school,
Bring a friend to school, clap, clap. (*Clap twice.*)

I brought a little friend,
My friend is a bear. (*Hold up a teddy bear and let the kids shout out what it is or say "Grr . . . grrr."*)
Bring a friend to school,
Bring a friend to school, clap, clap. (*Clap twice.*)
Bring a friend to school,
Bring a friend to school, clap, clap. (*Clap twice.*)

I brought a little friend,
My friend is an alligator. (*Hold up a toy alligator and have the kids shout out what it is, or hold up the Schmid book and point to the alligator, and/ or make alligator snaps with hands.*)
Bring a friend to school,
Bring a friend to school, snap, snap. (*Snap twice with hands forming an alligator mouth.*)
Bring a friend to school,
Bring a friend to school, snap, snap. (*Snap twice as before.*)

Picture Book

Rufus Goes to School by Kim T. Griswell. Illustrated by Valeri Gorbachev. Sterling, 2013.

- -

Rufus Leroy Williams III is frustrated because he cannot read. The little pig gets a backpack, leaves the farm, and enters a nearby school. The principal tells Rufus, "'No pigs in school!'" The principal thinks that pigs will track mud in the halls, make paper airplanes out of their artwork, and start food fights in the cafeteria. Rufus pleads, "'But I have a backpack'" to no avail. Rufus gets a lunchbox and tries again. The principal once again refuses. Rufus brings a blanket and convinces the principal that he will be a model student. The principal is still not convinced until Rufus pulls out his picture book. "'Ah!' Principal Lipid smiled. 'That makes a difference!'" Rufus is allowed to join school.

> **STORYTELLING TIPS:** Read this nice, long pattern story in an unhurried way. Let the kids repeat the principal's line "No pigs in school!"

Movement Activity

"If Pigs Went to Pig School" by Rob Reid.

- -

Have any picture book nearby. Instruct the children to shout out "READ A BOOK" with you when they see you hold one up.

If Pigs went to Pig School,
What would they learn?
They'd learn to oink, (*Make "oink" noises.*)
And wallow in the mud, (*Flop on the floor.*)
And even READ A BOOK! (*Hold up picture book.*)

If Elephants went to Elephant School,
What would they learn?
They'd learn to eat with their trunks, (*Hold up arm in front of nose.*)
And make trumpeting noises, (*Make elephant trumpet noise.*)
And even READ A BOOK! (*Hold up picture book.*)

If Turtles went to Turtle School,
What would they learn?
They'd learn to sun themselves on a log, (*Get low down on all fours.*)

And hide in their shell, (*Pull head into shoulders.*)
And even READ A BOOK! (*Hold up picture book.*)

Ask for suggestions from the audience of other animals to add to this pattern. Ask them for two characteristics they can act out.

Picture Book

Flip & Fin: We Rule the School! by Timothy Gill. Illustrated by Neil Numberman. Greenwillow, 2014.

- -

Two sand shark brothers tell jokes at school. Some are pretty bad, as one shark points out to his brother. "What did the sawfish see? He saw fish!" Flip keeps practicing for Joke Day. "What's the difference between a fish and a piano? You can't tuna fish." When it's his turn to perform at the assembly, Flip forgets his joke. His brother Fin comes to the rescue by yelling from the audience, "What kind of fish do you put in a peanut butter sandwich?" Flip recovers from his stage fright and says the punch line: "Jellyfish!"

> **STORYTELLING TIPS:** The last three pages of the book are filled with nearly twenty fish-related jokes. Choose your favorites to share with the kids (unless they *insist* on hearing all of them). My favorite is, "How are a goldfish and a grape alike? They are both purple, except for the goldfish."

Fingerplay

"Five Little Fish Heading to School" by Rob Reid.

- -

FIVE little fish were oh, so cool! (*Hold up five fingers.*)
These five fish were heading to school!
(*Make swimming motion with hands.*)
One little fish swam too close to shore, (*Point to thumb.*)

Now those five fish are down to . . .
(*Hold up five fingers and wiggle them . . .*)

FOUR little fish were oh, so cool!
(*. . . Tuck thumb and hold up four fingers.*)
These four fish were heading to school!
(*Make swimming motions with hands.*)
One little fish went far out to sea, (*Point to pinkie finger.*)
Now those four fish are down to . . .
(*Hold up four fingers and wiggle them . . .*)

THREE little fish were oh, so cool!
(*. . . Tuck pinkie finger with thumb and hold up three fingers.*)
These three fish were heading to school!
(*Make swimming motions with hands.*)
One little fish met a fishing crew, (*Point to ring finger.*)
Now those three fish are down to . . .
(*Hold up three fingers and wiggle them . . .*)

TWO little fish were oh, so cool!
(*. . . Tuck ring finger with thumb and pinkie and hold up last two fingers.*)
These two fish were heading to school!
(*Make swimming motions with hands.*)
One little fish jumped to the sun, (*Point to middle finger.*)
Now those two fish are down to . . .
(*Hold up two fingers and wiggle them . . .*)

ONE little fish was oh, so cool!
(*. . . Tuck middle finger with other fingers and hold up pointer finger.*)
That little fish was heading to school!
(*Make swimming motions with hands.*)
One little fish, it followed its heart, (*Point to heart.*)
That fish in school is oh, so smart! (*Point to head and nod.*)

Picture Book

Is Your Buffalo Ready for Kindergarten? by Audrey Vernick and Daniel Jennewein. Balzer & Bray, 2010.

- -

A little girl insists that if your buffalo has a backpack, then he is ready for kindergarten. "Is he feeling shy? That's okay. It can be hard to start something new. Especially when your buffalo will be the only one with horns. And a mane. Okay, and a hump. But who can resist that furry face?" Don't worry if it's too hard for him to use scissors or fit on the swings because, for show-and-tell, your buffalo can share that he is the state animal of Oklahoma. He'll have to learn to control his temper if another kid calls him "Fluppalo." And even though "he may be a tiny bit smelly," he'll be a super student.

> **STORYTELLING TIPS:** The book is a tongue-in-cheek universal primer of kindergarten behavior and experiences. Read the lines in a matter-of-fact style, as if the protagonist were a unique child instead of a buffalo. Relish lines such as these about snack time: "But he may be the only one who eats grass, then throws it up in his mouth and eats it again. Remember: everyone's special in his or her own way."

Closing Movement Activity

"Great Big Buffalo," traditional.

- -

Everyone stands. Connect this call-and-response camp song with the Vernick picture book. On the first lines, hold arms up and out wide at sides and hop in place. On the "far, far away" lines, point to the left, then center, and then right on each word and then hop up and down for "boo-boo-be-doo!"

Leader: Great big buffalo comin' round the mountains,
Audience: Great big buffalo comin' round the mountains,
Leader: Great big buffalo comin' round the mountains,

Audience: Great big buffalo comin' round the mountains,
Leader: Far, far away . . . boo-boo-be-doo!
Audience: Far, far away . . . boo-boo-be-doo!
Leader: Far, far away . . . boo-boo-be-doo!
Audience: Far, far away . . . boo-boo-be-doo!
Leader: Great big buffalo comin' round the mountains,
Audience: Great big buffalo comin' round the mountains,
Leader: Far, far away . . . boo-boo-be-doo!
Audience: Far, far away . . . boo-boo-be-doo!

Use little motions and a high voice for the next verse. Instead of holding arms out, hold up pointer fingers about an inch apart.

Leader: Teeny-tiny buffalo comin' round the mountains,
Audience: Teeny-tiny buffalo comin' round the mountains,
Leader: Teeny-tiny buffalo comin' round the mountains,
Audience: Teeny-tiny buffalo comin' round the mountains,
Leader: Far, far away . . . boo-boo-be-doo!
Audience: Far, far away . . . boo-boo-be-doo!
Leader: Far, far away . . . boo-boo-be-doo!
Audience: Far, far away . . . boo-boo-be-doo!
Leader: Teeny-tiny buffalo comin' round the mountains,
Audience: Teeny-tiny buffalo comin' round the mountains,
Leader: Far, far away . . . boo-boo-be-doo!
Audience: Far, far away . . . boo-boo-be-doo!

Use overly large motions and a loud, deep voice for the last verse.

Leader: Gi-gantic buffalo comin' round the mountains,
Audience: Gi-gantic buffalo comin' round the mountains,
Leader: Gi-gantic buffalo comin' round the mountains,
Audience: Gi-gantic buffalo comin' round the mountains,
Leader: Far, far away . . . boo-boo-be-doo!
Audience: Far, far away . . . boo-boo-be-doo!
Leader: Far, far away . . . boo-boo-be-doo!

Audience: Far, far away . . . boo-boo-be-doo!

Leader: Gi-gantic buffalo comin' round the mountains,

Audience: Gi-gantic buffalo comin' round the mountains,

Leader: Far, far away . . . boo-boo-be-doo!

Audience: Far, far away . . . boo-boo-be-doo!

5 Fun Backup Picture Books

Harry Goes to Dog School by Scott Menchin. Illustrated by the author. Balzer & Bray, 2012.

Harry doesn't want to be a boy. He wants to be a dog and goes around the house and yard on all fours, making dog noises and licking his sister instead of giving her a goodnight kiss. His parents enroll him in a dog school where he learns the basics: "Sit," "roll over," and "fetch." Harry doesn't like lunch, however. When he tried to engage his dog friends in human games, the dogs "didn't play like he did." Henry announces, "I think I'd like to be a boy again."

Hugs from Pearl by Paul Schmid. Illustrated by the author. HarperCollins, 2011.

Pearl the porcupine is excited about going to Wildwood School. She is a good friend because "she plays fair, shares her lunch treats, and best of all . . . Pearl LOVES to hug." Pearl's friends feel that her hugs are "just a little ouchy." Pearl designs a new outfit that allows her to give her friends hugs not once, but twice.

Kitty Cat, Kitty Cat, Are You Going to School? by Bill Martin Jr. and Michael Sampson. Illustrated by Laura J. Bryant. Two Lions, 2013.

Kitty Cat goes to school where he learns to sing, look at a book, count to ten and back again, play outside, eat treats, take a nap, share his bell at show-and-tell, and paint a picture of a heart. At the end of the school day, Kitty Cat says, "'Yes, yes, Teacher, and I had SO MUCH FUN!'"

Pete the Cat: Rocking in My School Shoes by Eric Litwin. Illustrated by James Dean. HarperCollins, 2011.

- -

Pete the Cat heads to school singing, "'I'm rocking in my school shoes, I'm rocking in my school shoes, I'm rocking in my school shoes.'" Throughout the day, Pete finds reasons to sing. He reads in his school shoes, eats in his school shoes, and plays in his school shoes. He even sings, paints, does addition, and writes in his school shoes. He tells his mother that he will rock in his school shoes tomorrow.

You're Wearing That to School? by Lynn Plourde. Illustrated by Sue Cornelison. Hyperion, 2013.

- -

A hippopotamus named Penelope decides to dress up for school wearing a "'sparkle rainbow outfit.'" Her friend Tiny says, "'You're going to wear THAT?'" Tiny helps Penelope pick more appropriate attire. Tiny also helps Penelope choose a sensible lunch (instead of an entire chocolate cake) and an item for show-and-tell (she wants to bring her stuffed hippo, but he instructs her to bring a rock). Penelope shows up the next day wearing her rainbow outfit and bringing her own stuffed hippo for show-and-tell.

LET'S VISIT THE ANIMALS

STORIES AND ACTIVITIES
ABOUT FIELD TRIPS

PROGRAM AT A GLANCE

★ Opening Picture Book: *Miss Fox's Class Earns a Field Trip* by Eileen Spinelli and Anne Kennedy

★ Picture Book: *Down by the Barn* by Will Hillenbrand

★ Sound Effects Rhyme: "The Farm Animals Introduce Themselves" by Rob Reid

★ Picture Book: *King of the Zoo* by Erica S. Perl and Jackie Urbanovic

★ Sound Effects Rhyme: "The Zoo Animals Introduce Themselves" by Rob Reid

★ Picture Book: *One Cool Friend* by Toni Buzzeo and David Small

★ Closing Musical Activity: "We're Taking a Walk in the Woods" by Rob Reid

Opening Picture Book

Miss Fox's Class Earns a Field Trip by Eileen Spinelli. Illustrated by Anne Kennedy. Albert Whitman, 2010.

- -

The children in Miss Fox's class hold a car wash, have a bake sale and a yard sale, and put on a play, all to raise money to go to Roller Coaster Planet amusement park. Unfortunately, much of the money they earn goes to pay Mr. Percy P. Possum when the kids accidentally spray him with water and ruin his clothes. They also break his glasses, break one of his teeth, and bust his yard gnome. In the end, Mr. Possum gives the kids the last twenty dollars they need. "I think it's safer to just give you the rest of the money." He then joins the class at Roller Coaster Planet.

> **STORYTELLING TIPS:** The text in this book is longer than I usually use for preschool storytime, but I've had great success with the young audience being patient, even throughout the addition and subtraction aspects of the fund-raising. You may feel inclined to rush. Don't. Just read at a normal pace.

Picture Book

Down by the Barn by Will Hillenbrand. Illustrated by the author. Two Lions, 2014.

- -

A tractor pulls a series of little wagons to gather farm animal infants one by one. The text is written to the tune of the traditional children's song "Down by the Station." The tractor heads out. "Down by the barn, early in the morning, see the little wagons all in a row! See the tractor driver pull his little lever . . . Puff, Puff, click, clank, OFF WE GO!" The first aboard is a calf. The train also picks up a chick, a piglet, a gosling, a lamb, a goat kid, and a kitten. The train finally arrives at the children's barn at the same time that a school bus with human children arrives. They all have gathered for storytime.

Sound Effects Rhyme

"The Farm Animals Introduce Themselves" by Rob Reid.

Pause before the italicized words and let the children in the audience fill in the proper animal sounds.

I am a Cow,
Yes, it's true.
I am a Cow
And I say, *"Moo!"*

I am a Horse,
And that's okay.
I am a Horse
And I say, *"Neigh!"*

I am a Sheep,
Well, la-de-da.
I am a Sheep
And I say, *"Baa!"*

I am a Duck,
And that's a fact.
I am a Duck
And I say, *"Quack!"*

I am a Chicken,
I'm not a Duck.
I am a Chicken
And I say, *"Cluck!"*

Picture Book

King of the Zoo by Erica S. Perl. Illustrated by Jackie Urbanovic. Orchard, 2013.

- -

Carlos the chameleon knows that he's the king of the zoo. "There was no one cooler or cleverer or charming-er than Carlos." He flips out when he spots a sign that reads "KANGAROO KING OF THE ZOO." He yells to the kangaroo that *he* is the king of the zoo. Signs appear that also proclaim the monkey, the elephant, the tiger, the giraffe, and the hippo are the kings of the zoo. When Carlos sarcastically asks, "Who else is king? The pygmy shrew?," he learns that it is indeed true. Carlos turns green with envy, then red with anger. He basks in a purple glow when he thinks of himself as king, but that turns to blue with sadness. He goes yellow with the fear that he is no longer king. When he overhears a girl exclaim that he is her favorite, Carlos changes into a multitude of colors and asks, "Who's still got it?"

STORYTELLING TIPS: Carlos goes through a range of emotions. The variety of his dialogue will be fun to read. Don't hold back.

Sound Effects Rhyme

"The Zoo Animals Introduce Themselves" by Rob Reid.

- -

As with the farm animal companion activity, pause before the italicized words and let the children in the audience fill in the proper animal sounds.

I am a Monkey,
Yes, it's true.
I am a Monkey
And I say, *"Ooh-ooh!"*

I am a Tiger,
Who you all adore.
I am a Tiger
And I say, *"Roar!"*

I am a Snake,
Look at this.
I am a Snake
And I say, *"Hiss!"*

I am an Owl,
I thought you knew.
I am an Owl
And I go, *"Whoo-whoo!"*

I am a Wolf,
I'm on the prowl.
I am a Wolf
And I go, *"Howl!"*

Picture Book

One Cool Friend by Toni Buzzeo. Illustrated by David Small. Dial, 2012.

Elliot, "a very proper young man" all dressed up in a suit, visited the aquarium with his father for Family Fun Day. "He skipped the mobs of kids at the Giant Saltwater Tank, Amazing Jellies Display, and Hands-On Tide Pool Exhibit" and headed for the penguin exhibit. He noticed that the penguins' tuxedo-like appearance was similar to his attire. Elliot sneaked the smallest penguin into his backpack and took it home. He cranked up the air conditioning and made an ice-skating rink in his bedroom. His father eventually learned about the penguin. We find out that the father has a tortoise companion that he found in the Galápagos Islands.

STORYTELLING TIPS: This book, too, has a long text. There are a lot of dialogue exchanges between Elliot and his father. They both speak in a formal tone that's fun to deliver. The long text will go quickly because of the contrasting "Grock" utterance of the penguin at one point as well as the father's shock of finding the penguin and uncharacteristically yelling, "ELLIOT!"

Closing Musical Activity

"We're Taking a Walk in the Woods" by Rob Reid.

Everyone stands. Sing to the tune of the traditional song "The Bear Went Over the Mountain." The melody can be found on the Internet as well as the following children's music recordings: *Animal Songs* by Susie Tallman (Rock Me Baby Records, 2012) and *Wee Sing Animals, Animals, Animals* by Pamela Beall and Susan Nipp (Price Stern Sloan, 1999). Tell the children that, after visiting the amusement park, the farm, the zoo, and the aquarium, they are going to take a nature hike. Place some chairs around the story program area to represent trees, boulders, and the like. If you are outside a story room, the bookshelves can represent the same things. Have the children move around in a single file to the styles reflected in your directions: first walking, then hopping, dancing, and jogging in place. After the jogging stanza, gather everyone together and whisper in a worried voice before continuing one final walk around the area.

We're taking a walk in the woods,
We're taking a walk in the woods,
We're taking a walk in the woods,
On this gorgeous day.

We're taking a hop in the woods,
We're taking a hop in the woods,
We're taking a hop in the woods,
On this gorgeous day.

We're doing a dance in the woods,
We're doing a dance in the woods,
We're doing a dance in the woods,
On this gorgeous day.

We're taking a jog in the woods,
We're taking a jog in the woods,
We're taking a jog in the woods,
On this gorgeous day.

We're scaring all the wildlife, (*Whisper.*)
We're scaring all the wildlife,
We're scaring all the wildlife,
If we hop, dance, and jog in the woods.

We're taking a walk in the woods,
We're taking a walk in the woods,
We're taking a walk in the woods,
On this gorgeous day.

5 Fun Backup Picture Books

Are the Dinosaurs Dead, Dad? by Julie Middleton. Illustrated by Russell Ayto. Peachtree, 2013.

Dave visits the museum with his father and asks the title question. The father assures his son that, yes, the dinosaurs are dead and proceeds to point out the qualities of the *Ankylosaurus* exhibit. The boy notices the dinosaur winking at him. His father tells him that it's just his imagination. Dave sees evidence of signs of life in the other museum dinosaurs. When the *Tyrannosaurus rex* follows them outside the museum and roars at them, the father states, "'THAT dinosaur's not dead!'"

Bailey at the Museum by Harry Bliss. Illustrated by the author. Scholastic, 2012.

Bailey the dog joins humans on a school bus going to the Museum of Natural History. The museum guide shows the class the dinosaur exhibits. Bailey loses control and tries to gnaw on a dinosaur bone. The teacher reminds him of the museum rules. "Dinosaur bones are *not* snacks!" Bailey gets separated from his class but uses his nose to locate them. "I smell Tommy's socks . . . and Sophie's bubble gum . . . and Mrs. Smith's perfume."

Duck to the Rescue by John Himmelman. Illustrated by the author. Holt, 2014.

Farmer Greenstalk doesn't know how he's going to get the pumpkins to the market. Duck overhears and hops in the truck. "Duck to the rescue!" Unfortunately, the pumpkins get smashed. "'I guess we can turn them into pumpkin pie,' said the farmer." Duck tries to help out by rescuing a calf, babysitting the chicks, comforting Emily at night, substituting for the scarecrow, and playing soccer. Each incident turns into disaster. Duck does succeed in finding cupcakes made by his sheep friend.

Fly Guy vs. the Flyswatter! by Tedd Arnold. Illustrated by the author. Scholastic, 2011.

- -

A pet fly named Fly Guy joins his boy owner Buzz on the class trip to the factory. Unfortunately for Fly Guy, the factory turns out to be The Fantastic Flyswatter Factory. Buzz and Fly Guy yell out "BAD NEWZZ!" The students get a demonstration of "the flyswatter of the future—the Super Swatter 6000!" The machine goes after a little fly. Fly Guy rescues the little fly, and the machine runs amok. The tour guide finally announces, "Everyone out! No more factory tours ever!"

Wild about You! by Judy Sierra. Illustrated by Marc Brown. Knopf, 2012.

- -

There's a new arrival at the zoo—an egg. The kangaroo claims it and places it in her pouch. A baby penguin hatches, and the kangaroo loves it. The pandas are gloomy until they find a little kitten. They adopt it and find it quite "pandalicious." Now, at this zoo, we know there is a "cool pandacat" as well as a "sweet pangaroo." Several other animal species help both the kangaroo and the pandas because "to bring up a baby . . . it takes a whole zoo!"

ANIMALS ON THE MOVE

STORIES AND ACTIVITIES
ABOUT TRANSPORTATION

- ★ Opening Picture Book: *Construction Kitties* by Judy Sue Goodwin Sturges and Shari Halpern

- ★ Picture Book: *Bug Patrol* by Denise Dowling Mortensen and Cece Bell

- ★ Sound Effects Activity: "Animal Sirens" by Rob Reid

- ★ Picture Book: *Big Bear's Big Boat* by Eve Bunting and Nancy Carpenter

- ★ Movement / Sound Effects Activity: "My Little Rowboat" by Rob Reid

- ★ Picture Book: *Ride, Fly Guy, Ride!* by Tedd Arnold

- ★ Musical Activity: "Hey! Hey! Fly Guy!" by Rob Reid

- ★ Closing Picture Book / Musical Activity: *The Wheels on the Bus* by Jeanne Willis and Adam Stower

Opening Picture Book

Construction Kitties by Judy Sue Goodwin Sturges. Illustrated by Shari Halpern. Holt, 2013.

These cute kittens are the least likely animal characters to wear hard hats and drive construction vehicles, but they get the job done. The kitties drive bulldozers, excavators, cranes, backhoes, and dump trucks. They also take a lunch break and eat sardines and drink milk. At the end of the day, we see that they've been building a new playground.

> **STORYTELLING TIPS:** Even though the book doesn't contain sound effects in the text, you can encourage the children to make heavy vehicle noises as well as music from a radio and eating noises ("munch, munch," "slurp," etc.).

Picture Book

Bug Patrol by Denise Dowling Mortensen. Illustrated by Cece Bell. Clarion, 2013.

Captain Bob of the Bug Patrol cruises along in his Bug Mobile. He gets an alarm call: "Code eleven. Donut swarm!" Bob makes several ants line up and show their manners while they eat. The second call comes in: "Beetles bumping at the mall." Bob makes the beetles hug each other after writing an accident report. Captain Bob also has to take care of racing spiders, transport striking roaches to the dump, and locate a missing flea. After breaking up a late-night party of chirping crickets (Bob puts them to sleep by playing a lullaby with his megaphone), Bob heads home "to my nest. And the bugs that I love BEST!"

> **STORYTELLING TIPS:** Teach the kids beforehand to make the repetitive police car siren noise that appears between incidents: "WEE-O! WEE-O! WEE-O! WOO! Bug Mobile coming through!"

Sound Effects Activity

"Animal Sirens" by Rob Reid.

- -

Have the kids pretend that other animals also have patrol cars inspired by the "WEE-O! WEE-O! WEE-O! WOO!" sound of the Bug Mobile. Ask them what kinds of siren sounds those cars might make. Here are some possibilities.

Mosquito Patrol: "BUZZ-O! BUZZ-O! BUZZ-O! BOO!"
Songbird Patrol: "TWEET-O! TWEET-O! TWEET-O! TOO!"
Duck Patrol: "QUACK-O! QUACK-O! QUACK-O! QU-OO!"
Fish Patrol: "BLUB-O! BLUB-O! BLUB-O! BOO!"
Monkey Patrol: "OOH-O! OOH-O! OOH-O! OOO!"

Picture Book

Big Bear's Big Boat by Eve Bunting. Illustrated by Nancy Carpenter. Clarion, 2013.

- -

Big Bear builds a big boat. "'I want it to be *just like* my little boat, but bigger.'" When it is finished, Big Bear pushes it into Huckleberry Lake. Beaver comes by and suggests the new boat needs a mast. Big Bear makes one. Otter swims by and points out the boat needs a top deck. Big Bear builds one. Huron flies overhead and tells Big Bear his boat needs a cabin. After Big Bear builds the cabin, he steps back to look at the boat. "'What an ugly big boat I've made. The mast leans over, the deck slants, and the cabin is higgledy-piggledy.'" Big Bear restores his big boat to its original condition.

> **STORYTELLING TIPS:** Read the book with a gentle tone throughout with a little vocal anxiety thrown in as Big Bear sees what he has done to his boat with the additions. After each of Big Bear's animal friends makes his or her suggestions, Big Bear says, "'Maybe you're right!'" This is a possible repetitive line for the audience to make.

Movement / Sound Effects Activity

"My Little Rowboat" by Rob Reid.

- -

Make rowing motions with arms throughout the activity.

My little rowboat,
Rowing round and round,
We rowed past a little frog,
It made this silly sound:
"Rib-it!" (*Everyone says "Rib-it."*)

My little rowboat,
Rowing round and round,
We rowed past a little duck,
It made this silly sound:
"Quack!" (*Everyone says "Quack."*)

My little rowboat,
Rowing round and round,
We rowed past a little goose,
It made this silly sound:
"Honk!" (*Everyone says "Honk."*)

My little rowboat,
Rowing round and round,
We rowed past a little fish,
It made this silly sound:
"Splash!" (*Everyone says "Splash."*)

My little rowboat,
Rowing round and round,
We rowed past a little turtle,
It made this silly sound:
"___" (*Shrug your shoulders.*)

Picture Book

Ride, Fly Guy, Ride! by Tedd Arnold. Illustrated by the author.
Scholastic, 2012.

- -

A boy has a pet fly called Fly Guy. "And Fly Guy could say the boy's name—BUZZ!" Buzz, his father, and Fly Guy go on a car trip. Everyone buckles up, including Fly Guy. Unfortunately, Fly Guy still gets sucked out of an open window and "into a passing truck." Buzz instructs his father to "'Follow that truck!'" While crossing a bridge, Fly Guy pops out of the truck and onto a motorboat. Buzz hollers, "'Follow that boat!'" The story continues with Fly Guy landing on a circus train, an airplane, and a rocket. Fortunately, Fly Guy falls off the rocket. All three ride home on a bicycle.

> **STORYTELLING TIPS:** Each time Buzz hollers, "Follow that . . .," pause and let the children fill in the appropriate mode of transportation based on the illustrations.

Musical Activity

"Hey! Hey! Fly Guy!" by Rob Reid.

- -

Sing to the tune of "Na Na Hey Hey Kiss Him Goodbye" by Steam, a song used at several ballparks. You can find the popular song on the Internet. Have everyone stand and wave their arms overhead as you sing.

Na Na Na Na!
Na Na Na Na!
Hey! Hey! Fly Guy!
Follow that truck! (*Have the kids pull an imaginary truck horn cord.*)
Follow that truck!
Hey! Hey! Fly Guy!

Follow that boat!

(Have the kids pretend they're steering the handle of a boat motor.)

Follow that boat!

Hey! Hey! Fly Guy!

Follow that plane!

(Have the kids move around with their arms out as wings.)

Follow that plane!

Hey! Hey! Fly Guy!

Na Na Na Na! *(Have the kids wave goodbye.)*

Na Na Na Na!

Go home! Fly Guy!

(End with a long, drawn-out buzzing noise that gets quieter and quieter.)

Closing Picture Book / Musical Activity

The Wheels on the Bus by Jeanne Willis. Illustrated by Adam Stower. Barron's, 2012.

Several animals make sound effects while heading to the zoo in a bus. "The wheels on the bus go round and round / Round and round, round and round / The wheels on the bus go round and round / at the zoo." The driver is a bear who goes "brum brum brum." His passengers include a penguin that goes "flip flap FLOP," a sick warthog going "snort snort SNEEZE," and a gang of crowded hippos going "squish squash SQUEEZE." Meanwhile, the tires on the bus go "hiss **BANG** POP!" throwing the creatures "upside down." This causes a meerkat to go "SLIP slip slide," a tiger to go "ROAR ROAR ROAR," a crocodile to go "SNAP SNAP SNAP," and a skunk to go "stink stink stink." While everybody clamors off, an owl goes "blink wink blink." An elephant goes "puff puff puff" and fills the tire with its trunk, causing all of the animals to "clap clap clap."

5 Fun Backup Picture Books

Big Mean Mike by Michelle Knudsen. Illustrated by Scott Magoon. Candlewick, 2012.

- -

Big Mean Mike is a tough dog who drives a big, mean car. One day, after buying a pair of combat boots "because they made his feet look extra big and mean," Mike discovers a "tiny, fuzzy bunny" in the trunk of the car "next to the big, tough spare tire." Mike sets the bunny on the sidewalk and takes off. The bunny shows up in Mike's glove compartment with a second bunny, upsetting Mike. The bunny keeps showing up with more friends. Mike lets them hang out with him but worries that the bunnies will ruin his image.

Go-Go Gorillas by Julia Durango. Illustrated by Eleanor Taylor. Simon & Schuster, 2010.

- -

Big Daddy, the king of the gorillas, sends his mouse messenger on a motorbike to summon all of the gorillas to the villa. "Go-go gorillas! Gotta go, gorillas, go!" The first gorilla heads to the king on his bike. The second gorilla heads out on a rowboat. Subsequent gorillas in this counting book travel by roller skates, a truck, the bus, a jalopy, a hot air balloon, a pogo stick, a taxicab, and a plane. They all meet a newborn princess named Priscilla. The last illustration shows Priscilla in a flying baby walker.

Hot Rod Hamster by Cynthia Lord. Illustrated by Derek Anderson. Scholastic, 2010.

A hamster shows up at a junkyard and tells the owner, "I need a hot rod!" They both look at a variety of car bodies. "Old car, new car, shiny painted blue car. Rust car, clean car, itty-bitty green car. Which would *you* choose?" Hamster chooses the green car. It's time to decide what kind of tires to put on the car. "Smooth wheels, stud wheels . . ." Each time a different component of the car is chosen, the text repeats the question to the reader, "Which would *you* choose?" Hamster is finally ready to roll. Be sure to read the opening sign announcing the hot rod race: "Sponsored by RUST-E-HYDRANTS."

My Little Train by Satomi Ichikawa. Illustrated by the author. Philomel, 2010.

A toy train chugs into Central Station. Several toy animals climb aboard and demand to be taken to several destinations. They go through tunnels (under a chair) making noise. "Quack quack, Baa baa, Grr grr, Ki ki ki, say all the happy passengers." They swing by a pond (a goldfish bowl), a field (a painting), the forest (a plant), and a mountain (a sofa). The train returns to the station with the last passenger, a young kangaroo looking forward to being reunited with its mother.

Number One Sam by Greg Pizzoli. Illustrated by the author. Hyperion, 2014.

A dog named Sam was the number-one car racer. Sam was used to winning, but when he finally lost a race, he was devastated. He became nervous during the next race and "was so distracted he missed the starting flag!" He quickly caught up to the other drivers. He was about to win when he saw five chicks crossing the road. Sam saved the chicks but finished the race in last place. Sam was happy to learn that, because of his actions, everyone thinks that he is number one.

ANIMAL CHEFS
STORIES AND ACTIVITIES ABOUT FOOD

PROGRAM AT A GLANCE

★ Opening Picture Book: *The Gingerbread Girl Goes Animal Crackers* by Lisa Campbell Ernst

★ Picture Book: *The Cow Loves Cookies* by Karma Wilson and Marcellus Hall

★ Sound Effects Activity: "Who Eats Corn?" by Rob Reid

★ Picture Book: *Seven Hungry Babies* by Candace Fleming and Eugene Yelchin

★ Movement Activity: "Five Little Hungry Birds" by Rob Reid

★ Picture Book: *The Watermelon Seed* by Greg Pizzoli

★ Movement Activity: "The Watermelon," traditional

★ Picture Book: *Worms for Lunch?* by Leonid Gore

★ Closing Imagination Exercise: "A Hungry Shark" by Rob Reid

Opening Picture Book

The Gingerbread Girl Goes Animal Crackers by Lisa Campbell Ernst.
Illustrated by the author. Dutton, 2011.

When the Gingerbread Girl opens her birthday present—a box of animal crackers—all of the animals run away. The Gingerbread Girl, as well as the old man and the old woman who baked her, gives chase. They are joined by neighboring farmers, a cow, a cat, a mouse, a flock of sheep, some children, chickens, and a scout troop. The animal crackers run into a cunning fox who promises to carry them safely across the river. The Gingerbread Girl helps the animal crackers get away from the hungry fox.

> **STORYTELLING TIPS:** The children in the audience will quickly learn the animal crackers' refrain, "We're wild Animal Crackers / Hear our fierce roar / You can't catch us / We're off to explore!" There are seven opportunities to say this rhyme.

Picture Book

The Cow Loves Cookies by Karma Wilson. Illustrated by Marcellus Hall.
Margaret K. McElderry, 2010.

The farmer knows what to feed all of his animals. He gives the horse some hay, the chickens some chicken feed, the geese cracked corn, the pigs gooey slop, and the dog gets doggy treats. The cow, however, only eats cookies. We learn why at the end of the book. The farmer

> **STORYTELLING TIPS:** As we learn what the farm animals eat, there is the repetitive line "the cow loves cookies." After you've read the line once or twice, on subsequent readings, pause after "the cow" and let the children say the rest of the line.

and the cow share a picnic lunch every day. "He takes cookies from a tin and Cow gives milk to dunk them in."

Sound Effects Activity

"Who Eats Corn?" by Rob Reid.

Leader: Who eats corn? Horses eat corn!

How does a horse say, "Yum! Yum?"

Audience: "Neigh, Neigh!"

Leader: Who eats corn? Cows eat corn!

How does a cow say, "Yum! Yum?"

Audience: "Moo, Moo!"

Leader: Who eats corn? Pigs eat corn!

How does a pig say, "Yum! Yum?"

Audience: "Oink, Oink!"

Leader: Who eats corn? Goats eat corn!

How does a goat say, "Yum! Yum?"

Audience: "Maa, Maa!"

Leader: Who eats corn? Chickens eat corn!

How does a chicken say, "Yum! Yum?"

Audience: "Cluck, Cluck!"

Leader: Who eats corn? Geese eat corn!

How does a goose say, "Yum! Yum?"

Audience: "Honk, Honk!"

Leader: Who eats corn? People eat corn!

How does a person say, "Yum! Yum?"

Audience: "Yum! Yum!"

Picture Book

Seven Hungry Babies by Candace Fleming. Illustrated by Eugene Yelchin. Atheneum, 2010.

Mama Bird works very hard to feed her babies. Seven hungry babies open their beaks wide. "'Feed us! Feed us!' the little ones cry." She flies off with a "Flappa-flap, swoop-swoop, zoom-zoom, yum!" and feeds the babies one by one. Poor Mama Bird is exhausted, but she manages to fly back and forth to satisfy each baby bird. One by one, the birds are fed and fall asleep. Just as she's ready to settle down, all seven birds wake up from their naps and demand to be fed again. Mama Bird decides, "It's Daddy's turn to fly."

> **STORYTELLING TIPS:** There are a lot of opportunities for the audience to chime in with repetitive lines. Have the children chant "Feed us! Feed us!" when you nod your head. Hold up the correct number of fingers to represent the number of birds left unfed throughout the storyline pattern. Ask the children to "gulp" when the baby birds get fed one by one. As you read about Mama Bird, reflect her progressive exhaustion with a weaker and weaker vocal delivery. Then, belt out the punch line about Daddy.

Movement Activity

"Five Little Hungry Birds" by Rob Reid.

Everyone stands.

Five little hungry birds, (*Flap arms as wings.*)
Looking for food to eat,
(*Look downward and move head back and forth.*)
One found a juicy worm, (*Pretend to grab the worm with beak.*)
Mmm . . . mmm . . . what a treat! (*Smile and rub belly.*)

Four little hungry birds, (*Flap arms as wings.*)
Looking for food to eat,
(*Look downward and move head back and forth.*)
One found a ripe blackberry, (*Pretend to grab the blackberry with beak.*)
Mmm . . . mmm . . . what a treat! (*Smile and rub belly.*)

Three little hungry birds, (*Flap arms as wings.*)
Looking for food to eat,
(*Look downward and move head back and forth.*)
One found a ripe red cherry, (*Pretend to grab the cherry with beak.*)
Mmm . . . mmm . . . what a treat! (*Smile and rub belly.*)

Two little hungry birds, (*Flap arms as wings.*)
Looking for food to eat,
(*Look downward and move head back and forth.*)
One found a sunflower seed,
(*Pretend to grab the sunflower seed with beak.*)
Mmm . . . mmm . . . what a treat! (*Smile and rub belly.*)

One little hungry bird, (*Flap arms as wings.*)
Looking for food to eat,
(*Look downward and move head back and forth.*)
It found a tasty bug, (*Pretend to grab the bug with beak.*)
Mmm . . . mmm . . . what a treat! (*Smile and rub belly.*)

No little hungry birds, (*Shake head and pat belly.*)
Looking for food to eat, (*Point to mouth and shake head again.*)
It won't be long before they're back, (*Flap "wings."*)
Looking for a tasty treat.
(*Look downward and move head back and forth.*)

Picture Book

The Watermelon Seed by Greg Pizzoli. Illustrated by the author. Hyperion, 2013.

- -

A watermelon-loving crocodile worries about swallowing a watermelon seed. "It's growing in my guts! Soon vines will come out of my ears!" He's also worried that he'll turn pink. His stomach starts to rumble and then out comes the seed with a loud "BUUUUUURR-RRRRPPP!!!" The crocodile vows to stop eating watermelon. "Well, maybe just a teeny, tiny bite."

> **STORYTELLING TIPS:** Roll your eyes so the young children in your audience can see that you think the crocodile's worries are full of nonsense. If it suits your personality, extend the burping noise for several seconds to reflect the way the word is laid out over two pages. While burping, signal with your hand for the children to join you. They can also help make the "Chomp! Chomp! Chomp!" lines as the crocodile rediscovers his love for watermelon.

Movement Activity

"The Watermelon," traditional.

- -

Everyone stands.

A watermelon is round (*Make circle with arms and hands.*)
And as hard as your head. (*Gently tap head.*)
The outside is green (*Mime holding a slice of watermelon.*)
And the inside is red. (*Nod.*)
A watermelon tastes good (*Mime taking a bite.*)
And is a juicy treat. (*Rub tummy.*)
But the seeds inside (*Open eyes very wide.*)
You do not eat. (*Mime spitting seeds.*)

Picture Book

Worms for Lunch? **by Leonid Gore. Illustrated by the author. Scholastic, 2011.**

The narrator asks "Who eats worms for lunch?" and starts off a chain reaction of responses from animals and one human child. A mouse states that it doesn't eat worms, it eats cheese. A cat appears and mentions it likes to eat mice or a bowl of milk. A cow gives milk, "'but I like to munch fresh green grass for lunch. Doesn't everyone?'" A chick prefers seeds over grass. Seeds are too dry for a bee. It prefers nectar from a flower. A girl wears an apron that states "I love spaghetti" but confides, "'And I love ice cream even more!'" A pelican prefers fish over ice cream. A monkey and a rabbit sitting in a boat wonder "What do fish like?" A fish ignores the two critters' bait of a banana and a carrot and states, "'Fish love wiggly, wiggly worms for lunch!'" The worm from the first page starts to leave the story, claiming, "'You can't eat me . . . I'm a character in this book!'"

> **STORYTELLING TIPS:** The book is full of lift-the-flap pages. Before turning the page, ask the kids in the audience if they know what type of food will be associated with each animal. Be sure to show the end of the book where the copyright information is located. There, we see the chick from the story who mentions, "'I like worms, too!'" After the entire story program is over, you might want to pull out a bag of gummy worms and ask, "*Who* eats worms for lunch?"

Closing Imagination Exercise

"A Hungry Shark" by Rob Reid.

Remind the children that there was a fish in the preceding picture book. What would that fish like to eat if it was a shark? Would it want to eat worms? Chant the following verse and then point to a child for a response. Repeat this imagination exercise as often as you like. When finished with several children's responses about their favorite food, ask the follow-up question. Don't be surprised if children have already blurted out what they think a shark likes to eat. Just ask them again.

A hungry shark wants to eat your food,
A hungry shark wants to eat your food,
A hungry shark wants to eat your food,
What's your favorite food? (*Example: Ice cream.*)
Will a hungry shark eat ice cream? (*Most children will yell out "No!" Some will yell out "Yes!" I speak from experience once again.*)
(*Follow-up question*) Well, what does a hungry shark like to eat?
(*Typical responses include fish and people.*)

5 Fun Backup Picture Books

The Duckling Gets a Cookie!? by Mo Willems. Illustrated by the author. Hyperion, 2012.

- -

The Pigeon is upset to learn that the Duckling got a cookie with nuts simply by asking for one. The Pigeon claims he has asked for things several times, including driving a bus. "But do I get what I ask for? NOOOOOOOOOOOOO!" The Duckling informs the Pigeon that he asked for the cookie so he could give it to the Pigeon. The Pigeon responds, "Hubba-Whaa?!?" The Pigeon leaves with the cookie, and the Duckling asks for another cookie. "But this time, no nuts."

Hands Off My Honey! by Jane Chapman. Illustrated by Tim Warnes. Little Tiger, 2013.

- -

Bear carries a pot of honey and warns all of the other forest animals, "It is all mine!" The tiny animals—Mouse, the Rabbit Brothers, and Mole—figure out a way to snitch a taste of honey. Once they succeed, Bear starts laughing. It turns out that this is a game they all play together. "'Big Scary Bear is my favorite game!' sighs Mole happily. 'Can we play it again, please?'" Bear gets up once more and starts roaring that he's got some food and he's not going to share—to the delight of the little critters.

If You Give a Dog a Donut by Laura Numeroff. Illustrated by Felicia Bond. Balzer & Bray, 2011.

- -

"If you give a dog a donut, he'll ask for some apple juice to go with it." When the juice is gone, he'll run outside to an apple tree to make more juice. Along the way, the dog will be distracted and play ball, do a dance, start a water fight, play pirate and go on a treasure hunt, and make a kite. When the kite gets tangled in the apple tree, it will remind the dog of apple juice. "And chances are, if he asks for some apple juice, he'll want a donut to go with it."

Little Mouse's Big Secret by Éric Battut. Illustrated by the author. Sterling, 2011.

- -

Mouse finds a single apple. "'It will be my secret.'" Mouse hides the apple by sticking it in the ground. One by one, different animals approach Mouse. "'What are you hiding?' asked Squirrel. 'It's my secret, and I'll never tell,' answered Mouse." Bird, Turtle, Hedgehog, Rabbit, and Frog ask the same question and get the same response. Mouse doesn't realize it, but an apple tree has been growing behind his back. When several apples fall to the ground, Mouse exclaims "'Uh-oh! My secret is out!'" The other animals eat the apples with Mouse, and we learn that sometimes "secrets are even better when you share them."

No More, Por Favor by Susan Middleton Elya. Illustrated by David Walker. Putnam, 2010.

- -

When Mamá Mono asks her son if he would like some fresh bananas—*plátanos frescos*—the little monkey, Monito, says, "'They taste sort of funky.'" Mamá sighs. "'Such a finicky monkey.'" Spanish and English words are interspersed throughout the book as different picky animal children refuse to eat the foods their mothers and fathers offer them. At the end of the story, the food that each child rejected is present at a picnic. The young animals enjoy their fruit *ensalada*. "And what could be better than sharing it? ¡Nada!" The Spanish words are bolded in the text; a glossary and a pronunciation guide are included.

ANIMALS FROM LONG AGO

STORIES AND ACTIVITIES ABOUT PREHISTORIC ANIMALS

- ★ Opening Picture Book: *Can I Bring Woolly to the Library, Ms. Reeder?* by Lois G. Grambling and Judy Love

- ★ Movement Activity: "The Woolly Mammoth," traditional; adapted by Rob Reid

- ★ Picture Book: *I'm Big!* by Kate McMullan and Jim McMullan

- ★ Movement Activity: "The Sauropod" by Rob Reid

- ★ Picture Book: *Rawr!* by Todd H. Doodler

- ★ Sound Effects Chant: "If a Dinosaur Says 'Roar!'" by Rob Reid

- ★ Picture Book: *The Three Triceratops Tuff* by Stephen Shaskan

- ★ Movement Activity: "The Triceratops" by Rob Reid

- ★ Closing Picture Book / Movement Activity: *I Am a Tyrannosaurus* by Anna Grossnickle Hines

Opening Picture Book

Can I Bring Woolly to the Library, Ms. Reeder? by Lois G. Grambling. Illustrated by Judy Love. Charlesbridge, 2012.

A boy brings a woolly mammoth into the public library. The mammoth receives its very own library card and charges into the children's room to "pick out a mammoth-sized stack of books to read." The librarian reminds the mammoth that there's no bellowing or thumping in the library. At the annual "Storybook Character Costume Party," the boy dresses as the Big Bad Wolf and the mammoth as Little Red Woolly Hood. At the end of the book, the mammoth heads back home to the North Pole, and the boy shows up at the library with a saber-toothed tiger.

> **STORYTELLING TIPS:** The boy tries to convince the librarian throughout the whole book that bringing a woolly mammoth into the library could work. Use a pleading voice for lines like "Can I? Please?" and an excited voice when the narrator explains the benefits of a mammoth, such as "he can reach the tall shelves with no problem."

Movement Activity

"The Woolly Mammoth," traditional; adapted by Rob Reid.

This activity is inspired by the traditional movement activity "An Elephant Goes Like This and That." Have everyone stand.

A woolly mammoth goes like this and that. (*Sway back and forth.*)
He's terribly huge, he's terribly fat.
(*Hold arms out to show the size of the mammoth.*)
Don't mess with Woolly, I hate to harp, (*Shake finger as if scolding.*)
But his tusks are very, very sharp!
(*Pull back finger quickly as if poked by a tusk.*)

Picture Book

I'm Big! by Kate McMullan. Illustrated by Jim McMullan. Balzer & Bray, 2010.

- -

A young sauropod (pronounced "sore-o-pod") oversleeps and is separated from its herd. It asks the reader (as well as other dinosaurs) for help. It stretches its neck "up, up, up" to take a look. Predators show up and scare the young dinosaur. It's too slow to run from danger, so it thinks "big" and states, "I'm a WHOLE LOTTA LIZARD!" The predators run away. The sauropod notices footprints that look familiar and finds its pack. "Everybody miss me?"

> **STORYTELLING TIPS:** The young dinosaur narrator has a playful voice, so assume a playful delivery with your vocals. For example, when the dinosaur stretches its neck, it says, "The weather up here? Sunny, with a chance of . . . PTEROSAURS! Chill, zoomers—just lookin' for my herd." *Pterosaurs* and *sauropod* are the only dinosaur names you'll have to practice saying aloud beforehand. The young dinosaur uses nicknames for the others: "stegs," "'saurs," and "dips" as well as "car-ni-vores."

Movement Activity

"The Sauropod" by Rob Reid.

- -

Everyone stands.

A sauropod's head (*Point to head.*)
Is way up high, (*Look upward.*)
It looks to me (*Point upward.*)
Like it touches the sky.
Its body is big (*Hold out arms in large semicircle.*)
And it's very strong, (*Make a muscle.*)
And its neck (*Point to neck.*)
Is very, very, very, very,
(*Put hands together and slowly move them apart vertically on each "very."*)

Very, very, very, very,
Very, very, very, very,
LONG!

Picture Book

Rawr! by Todd H. Doodler. Illustrated by the author. Scholastic, 2013.

- -

A young green dinosaur discusses how hard it is to be a dinosaur. It's bigger than the human children, bigger than the teachers, and even bigger than the school bus. The dinosaur worries about appearing too scary, but it's really nice and helpful. It even says "Excuse me" after it burps. The dinosaur realizes that humans get scared when it roars. However, people should realize that "RAAWWRRR" really means "Hello." It means "Good-bye," too!

> **STORYTELLING TIPS:** Read the dinosaur's lines with a mild-mannered delivery. That will make a nice contrast when the dinosaur roars. There's one double-page spread where the dinosaur roars in six different scenarios. Ask the kids to roar each time.

Sound Effects Chant

"If a Dinosaur Says 'Roar!'" by Rob Reid.

- -

Instruct the kids to make the noise of the dinosaur on the second line of each stanza as well as the translation on the fourth line.

If a dinosaur says, "Roar!"
If a dinosaur says, "Roar!"
It really means "I want more!"
It really means "I want more!"
(*Make an aside on this last line and say, "More friends, that is . . ."*)

If a dinosaur says, "Wobba-wobba-hey!"
If a dinosaur says, "Wobba-wobba-hey!"
It really means "Let's go out and play!"
It really means "Let's go out and play!"

If a dinosaur says, "Boogaloo!"
If a dinosaur says, "Boogaloo!"
It really means "I love you!"
It really means "I love you!"

If a dinosaur says, "Burp!"
If a dinosaur says, "Burp!"
Well . . . all it means is "Burp!"

Picture Book

The Three Triceratops Tuff by Stephen Shaskan. Illustrated by the author.
Beach Lane, 2013.

In this retelling of "The Three Billy Goats Gruff," three *Triceratops* brothers (Stanley Tuff, Rufus Tuff, and Bob Tuff) head out to "get some grub." They spot "lush vegetation" on the other side of the valley. Standing between them and their food is a *Tyrannosaurus rex*. Stanley, the littlest Tuff brother, heads down the valley with a "Clip, clomp. Clip, clomp. Clip, clomp." He convinces the *Tyrannosaurus rex* to wait for his bigger brother. The larger dinosaur tells Stanley, "'Then scram, squirt.'" Rufus Tuff, the middle brother, repeats the action, and finally, Bob Tuff, the largest Tuff brother, swats the

STORYTELLING TIPS: Teach the children to clap their hands on their legs and chant the repetitive phrase "Clip, clomp. Clip, clomp. Clip, clomp" at the appropriate times in the story. Have them say the chant louder with each Tuff brother.

Tyrannosaurus with his mighty tail. The *Tyrannosaurus* "was knocked clear out of the valley and never seen again."

Movement Activity

"The Triceratops" by Rob Reid.

- -

Everyone stands.

> The three-horned dino is called triceratops, (*Hold up three fingers.*)
> It has one horn in the middle, (*Point to your nose.*)
> And two more on top. (*Touch two spots on forehead.*)
> This dino doesn't flop, (*Sit and then stand again.*)
> This dino doesn't hop, (*Hop.*)
> 'Cause when it moves around, it goes clip-clop.
> (*Gallop around the room.*)

Closing Picture Book / Movement Activity

I Am a Tyrannosaurus **by Anna Grossnickle Hines. Illustrated by the author. Tricycle, 2011.**

- -

A young boy imitates the characteristics of a *Tyrannosaurus rex*, a *Velociraptor*, a *Brachiosaurus*, a *Triceratops*, and a *Pteranodon*. The last movement is the boy imitating a baby dinosaur hatching from an egg. The boy's mother joins the game, and he calls her "Maiasaura," which means "good mother lizard."

> **STORYTELLING TIPS:** Have the children stand as you read the story. They can roar when the boy roars, leap when the *Velociraptor* leaps, stretch high when the boy imitates the *Brachiosaurus,* hold their arms in front of their noses to imitate the *Triceratops,* and hold out their arms to fly like the *Pteranodon.* Instruct them to sit when the baby dinosaur "hatches" and enjoy the rest of the story.

5 Fun Backup Picture Books

How to Wash a Woolly Mammoth by Michelle Robinson. Illustrated by
Kate Hindley. Holt, 2014.

- -

A little girl gives a step-by-step guide for giving your woolly mammoth a bath. The first step is to fill the bathtub. "If your mammoth is thirsty, this may take a while." Step two is to add bubble soap to the bath. Step three is to add the mammoth. This, too, may take a while. The illustrations show the girl encouraging the mammoth to get into the tub by pushing it with a broom, scaring it with a mask, moving it closer via a skateboard, lifting it with a heavy-duty crane, and, finally, enticing it with cake. When the clean mammoth falls into a mud puddle, the girl gives the final step: "Throw in the towel and SNUGGLE!"

If I Had a Raptor by George O'Connor. Illustrated by the author.
Candlewick, 2014.

- -

A girl finds a box marked "FREE RAPTORS" and takes one home. She declares that baby raptors are cute because they are "funny and fluffy." As the raptor grows older, it tends to take on characteristics of a cat. It sharpens its claws on the furniture, it is fussy about its food, it sleeps all day, wakes the girl early in the morning, and eyes the birds outside. The girl concludes that a raptor would be "the best thing ever."

Me Want Pet! by Tammi Sauer. Illustrated by Bob Shea.
Simon & Schuster, 2012.

- -

Cave Boy has plenty of things: rocks, sticks, and a club. But what he really wants is a pet. He brings home a woolly mammoth. His mother complains Woolly is too big. Cave Boy next brings home a saber-toothed tiger. The tiger makes the other family members sneeze. Cave Boy brings home a dodo bird. Unfortunately, it's not potty trained. When a stampede of what looks like buffalos threatens everyone, the three animals come to the rescue. The family cheers "Phew-ga!" and Cave Boy finds himself with rocks, sticks, a club, and three pets. "Ooga!"

**Too Many Dinosaurs by Mercer Mayer. Illustrated by the author.
Holiday House, 2011.**

A boy's mother refuses his request for a dog. The boy picks up a dinosaur egg at a neighbor's yard sale for one dollar. When the egg hatches, the boy finds himself with a new pet *Triceratops*. The new pet causes problems by tearing up the garden, chasing dogs, and running away. The boy heads back to his neighbor and buys a dinosaur horn. When he blows the horn at the park, several dinosaurs appear, including a mean *Tyrannosaurus rex*. The boy blows the horn again, and the dinosaurs fade away. Mom insists that the boy get a puppy instead of a dinosaur.

**The Ugly Duckling Dinosaur: A Prehistoric Tale by Cheryl Bardoe.
Illustrated by Doug Kennedy. Abrams, 2011.**

In a "world of giant ferns, gingko trees, and dinosaurs," a mother duck wonders why a large egg doesn't hatch. When it finally does, the ducks screech and stare at what appears to be the ugliest duck ever. The young readers in the audience will know immediately that this new "duckling" is a young dinosaur. The newborn is sad and feels ugly. The mother duck takes care of the youngster despite the complaints from the neighbors. The ugly "duckling" protects his duck family from predators before finally finding other dinosaurs that look like him.

NOISY ANIMALS

STORIES AND ACTIVITIES
ABOUT SOUND EFFECTS

Opening Picture Book

Moo by David LaRochelle. Illustrated by Mike Wohnoutka. Walker, 2013.

The text consists almost entirely of variations of the word "moo." A cow sees a red car and takes it for a drive. She cruises along but panics when she hits a curve too fast. The car lands on top of a police car. The poor cow tries to explain what happened to the officer with a long series of "moo"s. She walks back home to the farm where she is confronted by the farmer, the car's owner. The cow quickly points to a nearby sheep and goes "Baaaaa!"

> **STORYTELLING TIPS:** There is a lot of interpretation on how to deliver the various "moo"s. I like to read the "MOO-moo" as if the cow were saying, "UH-oh!" When the cow is puttering in the car up and down hills, read the long, drawn-out "Moooooooooooooooo" with up and down lilts of your voice.

Sound Effects Activity

"A Cow Is Driving a Car" by Rob Reid.

Say the following little rhyme and then have the kids help break the pattern of the rhyme with the appropriate animal noises. Have them go wild when making the noises, similar to when the cow in LaRochelle's picture book *Moo* responds to the police officer.

A cow is driving, "Moo! Moo! Moo!"
A cow is driving, "Moo! Moo! Moo!"
A flock of ducks think, "Let's drive, too!"
A flock of ducks think, "Let's drive, too!"
This is how it sounds to you:
"Quack! Quack! Quack! Quack! Quack!
Quack! Quack! Quack! Quack! Quack!"

A cow is driving, "Moo! Moo! Moo!"
A cow is driving, "Moo! Moo! Moo!"
A herd of sheep think, "Let's drive, too!"
A herd of sheep think, "Let's drive, too!"
This is how it sounds to you:
"Baa! Baa! Baa! Baa! Baa!
Baa! Baa! Baa! Baa! Baa!"

A cow is driving, "Moo! Moo! Moo!"
A cow is driving, "Moo! Moo! Moo!"
A pack of mules think, "Let's drive, too!"
A pack of mules think, "Let's drive, too!"
This is how it sounds to you:
"Hee-haw! Hee-haw! Hee-haw! Hee-haw! Hee-haw!
Hee-haw! Hee-haw! Hee-haw! Hee-haw! Hee-haw!"

A cow is driving, "Moo! Moo! Moo!"
A cow is driving, "Moo! Moo! Moo!"
A parcel of pigs think, "Let's drive, too!"
A parcel of pigs think, "Let's drive, too!"
This is how it sounds to you:
"Oink! Oink! Oink! Oink! Oink!
Oink! Oink! Oink! Oink! Oink!"

A cow is driving, "Moo! Moo! Moo!"
A cow is driving, "Moo! Moo! Moo!"
A gang of turkeys think, "Let's drive, too!"
A gang of turkeys think, "Let's drive, too!"
This is how it sounds to you:
"Gobble! Gobble! Gobble! Gobble! Gobble!
Gobble! Gobble! Gobble! Gobble! Gobble!"

A cow is driving, "Moo! Moo! Moo!"
A cow is driving, "Moo! Moo! Moo!"
A swarm of bees think, "Let's drive, too!"

A swarm of bees think, "Let's drive, too!"
This is how it sounds to you:
"Buzz! Buzz! Buzz! Buzz! Buzz!
Buzz! Buzz! Buzz! Buzz! Buzz!"

Picture Book

Froodle by Antoinette Portis. Illustrated by the author. Roaring Brook, 2014.

- -

Every day throughout the year, the crow goes "Caw," the dove says "Coo," the cardinal goes "Chip," and the brown bird sings "Peep." One day, the brown bird says, "Froodle sproodle." Crow is not amused and demands that the little bird say "Peep." The brown bird follows up with "Tiffle baffle, just a little miffle," and the rest of the birds experiment with their own sounds. "The neighborhood was never the same."

> **STORYTELLING TIPS:** Look startled every time the brown bird makes its strange, un-birdlike noises.

Cheer

"The Mosquito Wave" by Rob Reid.

- -

To prepare the kids for the following Virginia Kroll book, lead them in a cheer, as if they were at a sporting event.

Leader: Give me an M!
Audience: M!
Leader: Give me an O!
Audience: O!
Leaders: Give me an S!
Audience: S!

Leader: Give me a Q!

Audience: Q!

Leader: Give me a U!

Audience: U!

Leader: Give me an I!

Audience: I!

Leader: Give me a T!

Audience: T!

Leader: Give me another O!

Audience: O!

Leader: What does it spell?

Audience: MOSQUITO!

Leader: What does it spell?

Audience: MOSQUITO!

Leader: What does it spell?

Audience: MOSQUITO!!! (*Have everyone scream and wave their hands frantically as if waving away a pesky mosquito.*)

Picture Book

***Mosquito* by Virginia Kroll. Illustrated by Betsy LePlatt. Pelican, 2011.**

A mosquito approaches several animals with a "Buzz." Each animal responds angrily with a variety of phrases. Some of the more clever wordplay shows up when Moose bellows, "Vamoose!," Hare thumps, "Dagnabbit," Mole squeaks, "Holy moly," Deer sighs, "Dear me," and Squirrel screeches, "Oh, nuts!" The mosquito finally encounters a bat. "'Gulp, gulp!' went Bat. And that was that!"

> **STORYTELLING TIPS:** Every page begins with Mosquito buzzing. Teach the children to make this sound with every new page.

Picture Book

Tiptoe Joe by Ginger Foglesong Gibson. Illustrated by Laura Rankin. Greenwillow, 2013.

- -

Tiptoe Joe is a sneaker-wearing bear with a secret. Joe is joined by Donkey, who goes "CLOP, CLOP," Rabbit, who goes "THUMP, THUMP," and Turkey with its "FLAP, FLAP." The animals follow Tiptoe Joe to learn his secret. Three more animals join them: Moose ("THUD, THUD"), Owl ("SWISH, SWISH"), and Beaver ("SLAP, SLAP"). The animals continue to follow Tiptoe Joe, pleading, "What's the secret? Let us know?" The last illustration reveals Tiptoe Joe's secret: two newborn, sleeping bear cubs.

> **STORYTELLING TIPS:** Encourage the children to repeat the sound effects noises found throughout the text ("CLOP, CLOP," "THUMP, THUMP," etc.).

Movement Activity

"Animals Move" by Rob Reid.

- -

Have everyone stand. Tell them that many times we make the sounds an animal makes with its mouth. This time, we're going to make the sounds an animal makes when it moves. Have the children move in a circle. Call out "Elephant" and then "Stomp! Stomp!" Ask them to make that noise and to demonstrate how an elephant moves. Call out a different animal after they complete a circle.

Elephant: Stomp! Stomp!
Bird: Flap! Flap!
Snake: Slither! Slither!
Bunny: Thump! Thump!
Fish: Swish! Swish!

Closing Picture Book / Musical Activity

The Wheels on the Bus by Jane Cabrera. Illustrated by the author.
Holiday House, 2011.

- -

A bus is filled with animal passengers and a giraffe driver. The lion roars, the flamingoes flap, the zebra chomps, the monkeys chatter, the hyena laughs, the crocodile snaps, and the bush babies snore. The bus finally arrives at its destination: a watering hole where everyone goes "SPLISH! SPLASH! SPLOSH! All day long!"

> **STORYTELLING TIPS:** Sing the text to the tune of the traditional song "The Wheels on the Bus." The melody can be found on the Internet as well as the following children's music recordings: *Early Childhood Classics* by Hap Palmer (Hap-Pal Music, 2000) and *Rise and Shine* by Raffi (Troubadour, 1982). There is a music score at the end of the book as well. The children can contribute the noises the animals make even if they don't join in with the rest of the song. Encourage them to add motions as well. For example, when the monkeys chatter, the kids can wave their arms in the air. When the crocodile snaps, the children can clap their hands.

5 Fun Backup Picture Books

Be Quiet, Mike! by Leslie Patricelli. Illustrated by the author.
Candlewick, 2011.

- -

Mike the monkey started drumming inside his mother even before he was born. He went "KICK THUMP POW KICK THUMP POW." As a toddler, he was always playing with his fingers and feet with a "beat, beat, beat." Unfortunately, Mike only hears one thing over and over: "BE QUIET, MIKE!" He tried to be quiet, but "he couldn't stop tapping." Mike makes a homemade drum set out of pans, buckets, and silverware. He goes "DIGGETY DIGGETY ZAT ZOOM CRASH! COFFEE CAN COFFEE CAN POT PAN SPLASH!" Mike is surprised that his new sounds bring about applause. His family now shouts, "PLAY LOUDER, MIKE!"

Bow-Wow Wiggle-Waggle by Mary Newell DePalma. Illustrated by the author. Eerdmans, 2012.

A boy is playing with his dog when a cat appears. The two animals run away with a "FLEE, FLY FLUTTER-FLUTTER FLICKER, FLASH." They all encounter a frog, some geese, a snake, a rabbit, and a squirrel. The dog realizes that it is lost and goes, "sag, flag sniffle-snuffle sputter bawl." When the dog is reunited with its owner, there is a "HUG, SNUG, TUMBLE, CUDDLE, PET, PAT . . . PLAY!"

Pig Has a Plan by Ethan Long. Illustrated by the author. Holiday House, 2012.

Pig wants to nap. Unfortunately his rest is interrupted when Hen saws a piece of wood, Cow gabs on her cell phone, Cat pops the mice's balloons, Dog hammers, Rat uses a mixer, Hog hums, Pup dances to the radio, and Fly sips soda. Pig hides deeper in the mud, not realizing at first that the other animals are throwing a birthday party in his honor.

Thumpy Feet by Betsy Lewin. Illustrated by the author. Holiday House, 2013.

When a cat walks, it makes a "Thumpy thumpy" noise. It smells food. "MMMMMMmmmmmmm." The cat smacks its lips over and over and then gives itself several licks. "Licky licky." It next plays with a toy mouse. "POUNCY POUNCE!" The cat flips the mouse up in the air with a "Flippy Flip flip flip flippy flippy flip." The cat then yawns, nods, snoozes. The last illustration shows the cat playing with a ball of yarn. "LOOKY LOOK!"

What's Your Sound, Hound the Hound? by Mo Willems. Illustrated by the author. Balzer & Bray, 2010.

- -

Cat asks the title question to a dog pulling a tray of bone cookies out of an oven. Dog replies with "WOOF! WOOF! WOOF!" Cat asks, "What's your sound?" to Chick the Chick and Cow the Cow, and they also reply. When Cat asks, "What's your sound Bunny the Bunny?," the poor rabbit looks upset. No one is sure what Bunny's sound is. Finally, all of the animals realize that Bunny "sounds like somebody needs a hug!"

A NEW LOOK AT OLD FAVORITES

STORIES AND ACTIVITIES ABOUT
FRACTURED FAIRY TALES

Opening Fairy Tale Quiz by Rob Reid

Inform your audience that the stories in this program are all slightly mixed-up from the stories they might normally know. Tell them you're going to make a series of statements to see how well they know their fairy tales. They have to tell you what's wrong with the stories or plots described.

> Sleeping Beauty huffs and puffs outside the houses of the Three Little Pigs. (*The Big Bad Wolf huffs and puffs.*)
> Jack climbs the beanstalk and finds the seven dwarfs at the top. (*Jack finds the giant at the top of the beanstalk.*)
> The Three Billy Goats Gruff walk over the bridge of the Ugly Duckling. (*The Three Billy Goats Gruff walk over the bridge of the troll.*)
> The Fairy Godmother turns the three bears into a beautiful princess. (*The Fairy Godmother turns Cinderella into a beautiful princess.*)

Praise your audience for passing the quiz and knowing their fairy tales.

Picture Book

The Great Fairy Tale Disaster by David Conway. Illustrated by Melanie Williamson. Tiger Tales, 2012.

- -

The Big Bad Wolf is tired of huffing and puffing at the houses of the Three Little Pigs and goes off seeking a new fairy tale. He takes over Cinderella's role but dislikes wearing dresses. The wolf climbs Jack's beanstalk but finds the giant's "Fee, Fie, Fo, Fum" chant too scary. He chases Sleeping Beauty away but is upset to get a kiss from the handsome prince. The wolf also makes appearances in the stories of "Goldilocks and the Three Bears," "Rapunzel," "The Three Billy

> **STORYTELLING TIPS:** The wolf's dialogue is fun in itself. Play around with his lines, particularly when he tells Sleeping Beauty, "WAKEY! WAKEY! Out you go!"

Goats Gruff," "Snow White and the Seven Dwarfs," "Hansel and Gretel," and "Puss in Boots." The fairy tale characters became confused and "there was chaos and confusion everywhere!" Everything becomes right once more when the Big Bad Wolf rejoins the three pigs and splashes down into the pot of hot water. Well, for everyone but the wolf, who cries, "Oooh, not again!"

Fingerplay

"Hickory, Dickory, Dock, the Wolf Ran Up the Clock," traditional; adapted by Rob Reid

----

Everyone stands.

> Hickory, dickory, dock, (*Stand straight and make bodies into clocks.*)
> The wolf ran up the clock. (*Make two fingers "run" up the "clock."*)
> The clock struck one, (*Strike hands one time overhead.*)
> The wolf howled and THEN ran down. (*Howl and then make fingers "run" down the "clock."*)
> Hickory, dickory, dock.

Picture Book

The Three Bully Goats by Leslie Kimmelman. Illustrated by Will Terry. Albert Whitman, 2011.

> Three bully goats named Gruff, Ruff, and Tuff make trouble for the poor little ogre who lives under the bridge. The goats cross the bridge

STORYTELLING TIPS: Because most ogres are mean, read Little Ogre's lines with a meek voice for contrast. Read the progressive goats' lines with deeper and meaner voices. Also, teach the kids in the audience to slap their legs when the goats go "Trip trap trip trap trip trap" over the bridge.

and immediately head-butt the woodland animals. Little Ogre comes up with a plan after the largest goat threatens him. Little Ogre tells the goat to head over to the tall grass because it's the tastiest. The mean goat head-butts several baby skunks. The skunks, of course, raise their tails and let the mean goats have it. "What a smell. What a stench. What a way to pay those bullies back!"

Fingerplay

"Three Little Billy Goats Trip Trap Trip," traditional; adapted by Rob Reid.

- -

Recite the words in the same cadence as the popular fingerplay "Five Little Monkeys Jumping on the Bed." To learn the cadence, you can view folks performing that fingerplay on the Internet. Tell the kids to pretend they are the ogre beneath the bridge and they hear the Three Billy Goats Gruff overhead.

Three little billy goats
Trip-trap-trip.
(*Hold up three fingers and have them bounce up and down.*)
One ran across
At a real fast clip. (*Hold up one finger and move it quickly in front of you from one side to the other.*)
Ogre called its Mama and the Mama yipped,
(*Pretend to make a phone call.*)
"No more billy goats trip-trap-trip!" (*Wag finger as if scolding.*)

Two little billy goats
Trip-trap-trip, (*Hold up two fingers and have them bounce up and down.*)
One ran across
At a real fast clip. (*Hold up one finger and move it quickly in front of you from one side to the other.*)
Ogre called its Mama and the Mama yipped,
(*Pretend to make a phone call.*)
"No more billy goats trip-trap-trip!" (*Wag finger as if scolding.*)

One little billy goat

Trip-trap-trip, (*Hold up one finger and have it bounce up and down.*)

He ran across

At a real fast clip. (*Hold up one finger and move it quickly in front of you from one side to the other.*)

Ogre called its Mama and the Mama yipped,

(*Pretend to make a phone call.*)

"No more billy goats trip-trap-trip!" (*Wag finger as if scolding.*)

Picture Book

Goldilocks and the Three Dinosaurs by Mo Willems. Illustrated by the author. Balzer & Bray, 2012.

- -

Papa Dinosaur, Mama Dinosaur, "and some other Dinosaur who happened to be visiting from Norway" lay a trap in their house in case an "innocent little succulent child happens by." They hide in the trees and observe Goldilocks head into their home. Instead of porridge, the dinosaurs made chocolate pudding. Goldilocks eats it all up, even the hot and cold bowls. The dinosaurs, of course, have a fondness for "delicious chocolate-filled-little-girl-bonbons." Goldilocks finds the chairs too large before realizing she has stumbled into the dinosaurs' home and not the bears' house. She runs out the back door as the dinosaurs rush in through the front door. Unfortunately for the dinosaurs, they learn a hard lesson: "LOCK THE BACK DOOR!"

> **STORYTELLING TIPS:** Mo Willems decorated the endpapers with ideas for other Goldilocks books and crosses them all out. Be sure to share some of them with your audience members after reading the book. Some of my favorites include "Goldilocks and the Three Bus Drivers," "Goldilocks and the Three Musketeers," "Goldilocks and the Rocket Scientists," and "Goldilocks and the Three Foot-Long Hoagies."

Musical Activity

"Goldilocks" by Rob Reid.

Sing to the tune of "Over in the Meadow." The melody can be found on the Internet as well as the following children's music recordings: *Animal Songs* by Susie Tallman (Rock Me Baby Records, 2012) and *Wee Sing Nursery Rhymes and Lullabies* by Pamela Beall and Susan Nipp (Price Stern Sloan, 1985). This musical activity first appeared in *LibrarySparks* magazine.

Goldilocks went to the home of the bears,
She decided to sample their wares,
She ate their porridge and then she cried,
"It's too hot!"
(*Make an expression as if you ate something hot while fanning mouth.*)
"It's too cold!"
(*Scrunch face, hug self, and shake whole body as if shivering.*)
And then, "It's just right!"
(*Make a circle with thumb and pointer finger and wink.*)

Goldilocks went to the home of the bears,
She decided to sample their wares,
She sat on their chairs and then she cried,
"It's too hard!" (*Rub bottom as if it is sore.*)
"It's too soft!" (*Hold arms overhead and wiggle downward as if sinking.*)
And then, "It's just right!"
(*Make a circle with thumb and pointer finger and wink.*)

Goldilocks went to the home of the bears,
She decided to sample their wares,
She crawled into their beds and then she cried,
"It's too hard!" (*Hold body stiff as a board with arms alongside.*)
"It's too soft!" (*Repeat the motions you did for the soft chair.*)
And then, "It's just right!" (*Pretend to fall asleep.*)

Goldilocks slept in the home of the bears,
She didn't hear them climbing up the stairs,
They woke her up and then she cried, (*Pause.*)
"AAAAAAAAAAHHHHHHHH!!!!!" (*Everyone screams.*)

Picture Book

I Don't Want to Be a Pea! by Ann Bonwill. Illustrated by Simon Rickerty. Atheneum, 2012.

- -

Hugo the hippo and Bella the bird dress up for the "Hippo-Bird Fairy-Tale Fancy Dress Party" (or, as Bella corrects Hugo, the "BIRD-HIPPO Fairy-Tale Fancy Dress Party"). Hugo decides to go as the princess from the fairy tale "The Princess and the Pea." Unfortunately, Bella refuses to dress as the pea. She decides instead the two should attend as a mermaid and her rock. Hugo counters that they should be a king and his jester. Bella prefers to appear as Cinderella with Hugo as her pumpkin. The two go their separate ways but miss each other. They finally head to the party as Bella's hippo and Hugo's bird.

STORYTELLING TIPS: Show a photo of a real hippo with a bird sitting on its head. Mention that in nature, birds and hippos have a close relationship. This is a fun book to read with a partner, each trading lines between Hugo and Bella.

Closing Fingerplay

"The Not-So-Itsy-Bitsy Hippo," traditional; adapted by Rob Reid.

- -

Make large, oversized versions of the traditional "Itsy-Bitsy Spider" fingerplay motions, as well as loud sounds. Rush the "Not-So-Itsy-Bitsy Hippo" lines to add to the comedic effect.

The Not-So-Itsy-Bitsy Hippo went up the water spout.

(*Walk fingers upward.*)

Down came the rain and washed the hippo out.

(*Wiggle fingers downward.*)

Out came the sun and dried up all the rain.

(*Make a circle with hands overhead.*)

And the Not-So-Itsy-Bitsy Hippo went up the spout again.

(*Walk fingers upward again.*)

5 Fun Backup Picture Books

Cinderelephant by Emma Dodd. Illustrated by the author. Scholastic, 2012.

A poor elephant is forced to do the chores for two horrible cousins known as the Warty Sisters (they are warthogs). Prince Trunky sends invitations for the ball to all of the girls in the neighborhood. After the Warty Sisters leave poor Cinderelephant alone at home, a Furry Godmouse grants a wish. "You shall go to the ball!" Cinderelephant dances with the prince until the clock strikes midnight. Prince Trunky tracks her down with the fabulous shoe she left behind. "And, of course, they were hugely happy ever after."

Goldilocks and Just One Bear by Leigh Hodgkinson. Illustrated by the author. Nosy Crow, 2011.

A lost bear seeks refuge in Snooty Towers. He finds a snack, a comfortable beanbag chair, and a bed for a nap. A man, a woman, and their child find that someone has been nibbling from the fishbowl, the little boy's toast, and "dear Little Pumpkin's kitty nibbles." The trio then notices that the boy's beanbag chair has been popped. They spot the bear when the mommy person asks, "Baby Bear?" The bear recognizes the mommy person as Goldilocks, all grown up. They celebrate their reunion with some porridge that's not too hot, not too cold, but just right.

Honestly, Red Riding Hood Was Rotten! The Story of Little Red Riding Hood as Told by the Wolf by Trisha Speed Shaskan. Illustrated by Gerald Guerlais. Picture Window Books, 2012.

This version of the traditional fairy tale is told from the wolf's perspective. The hungry wolf meets the conceited Little Red in the woods. When she tells him about her visit to Granny's house, the wolf envisions "Granny for breakfast, Little Red for lunch." The wolf gets to Granny's house and chomps her down. "She was no McIntosh apple, but not too bad." Little Red arrives and commences to talk about her own beauty. The wolf gulps her down as well.

Maria Had a Little Llama / María tenía una llamita by Angela Dominguez. Illustrated by the author. Holt, 2013.

High in the Peruvian mountains, "Maria had a little llama whose fleece was as white as snow / María tenía una llamita cuya lana era tan blanca como la nieve." This bilingual retelling of the classic nursery rhyme "Mary Had a Little Lamb" shows the children laughing at the llama that followed Maria to school.

The Three Ninja Pigs by Corey Rosen Schwartz. Illustrated by Dan Santat. Putnam, 2012.

Three little pigs learn the martial arts in order to defeat the wolf that goes around town blowing houses down. Pig One enrolls at the new Ninja school to learn the art of aikido but drops out because he's bored with the drills. Pig Two takes jujitsu but doesn't study enough. Pig Three becomes a master of karate. "By the time she was through, she could break boards in two by performing a perfect pork chop!" The first two pigs lose their battles with the wolf, but Pig Three scares the wolf with her moves. "And life was forever wolf-free."

ANIMAL WINTER WONDERLAND
STORIES AND ACTIVITIES ABOUT WINTER

Opening Picture Book

If It's Snowy and You Know It, Clap Your Paws! by Kim Norman. Illustrated by Liza Woodruff. Sterling, 2013.

Several forest friends frolic in the snow to the tune of the traditional song "If You're Happy and You Know It." A polar bear slides down a hill on its stomach with a rabbit perched on top as if riding a toboggan. "If it's snowy and you know it, clap your paws. You can tumble on the tundra, just because. If it's snowy and you know it, roll a snowball up and throw it. If it's snowy and you know it, clap your paws." The animals also taste a snowflake, grab their skis, make snow sculptures of their friends, build a snow fort, roar, blow a kiss, share a meal, and soak their toes before seeking shelter for indoor activities.

STORYTELLING TIPS: Before sharing the book, ask the children to pretend they are an animal and practice clapping their paws. Sing or chant the text that uses the tune of the traditional song "If You're Happy and You Know It." The melody can be found on the Internet as well as the following children's music recordings: *Bob's Favorite Sing Along Songs* by Bob McGrath (Bob's Kids Music, 2012) and *Let's Play* by Raffi (Troubadour, 2002). Encourage the kids to act out what the animals are doing for each stanza (catching snowflakes with their tongues, miming skiing, roaring, etc.). It's okay to stop and start the melody to allow the children to perform these various tasks.

Picture Book

Old Bear and His Cub by Olivier Dunrea. Illustrated by the author. Philomel, 2010.

Old Bear loves Little Cub "with all his heart." Little Cub loves Old Bear. However, when Old Bear tells Little Cub to eat his porridge, Little Cub says, "No, I won't." The two have a brief standoff before

Little Cub complies. The same thing happens when Old Bear tells Little Cub to wear his scarf outside in the winter weather. "'No, I won't,' said Little Cub. 'Yes, you will,' said Old Bear." Little Cub wears his scarf. The two go back and forth on other issues until their roles reverse. Little Cub tells Old Bear to wear a scarf as well. "'No, I won't,' said Old Bear." Old Bear gets sick and crawls into bed. Little Cub makes blackberry tea, which Old Bear refuses to drink at first, and reads a story. They both fall asleep in the bed.

> **STORYTELLING TIPS:** Because this is a story about a battle of wills, speak each commanding line of Old Bear and Little Cub with a stern look on your face. Soften that look when you read the repetitive lines "Old Bear loved Little Cub with all his heart" and "Little Cub loved Old Bear with all *his* heart."

Movement Activity

"Old Bear and Little Cub" by Rob Reid.

Do this activity twice. Give verbal instructions the first time through. The kids will quickly learn their parts and have even more fun the second time through.

Little Cub, you must eat your food. (*Wag finger at the audience.*)
No, I won't.
No, I won't.
No, I won't. (*Audience crosses their arms and shakes their heads.*)
Little Cub, you must eat your food.
Oh, okay, I will. (*Audience mimes eating food.*)

Little Cub, you must wear your scarf. (*Wag finger at the audience.*)
No, I won't.
No, I won't.

No, I won't. (*Audience crosses their arms and shakes their heads.*)

Little Cub, you must wear your scarf.

Oh, okay, I will. (*Audience mimes wrapping scarves around their necks.*)

Little Cub, you must go to bed. (*Wag finger at the audience.*)

No, I won't.

No, I won't.

No, I won't. (*Audience crosses their arms and shakes their heads.*)

Little Cub, you must go to bed.

Oh, okay, I will. (*Audience puts heads on hands.*)

Big Bear, you must read another book.

(*Audience wags fingers at storyteller.*)

No, I won't.

No, I won't.

No, I won't. (*Storyteller crosses her arms and shakes her head.*)

Big Bear, you must read another book.

Oh, okay, I will. (*Storyteller smiles and pulls out the next book to read.*)

Picture Book

No Two Alike by Keith Baker. Illustrated by the author. Beach Lane, 2011.

- -

"No two snowflakes are alike, almost, *almost,* but not quite." Baker goes on to show us that no two nests, tracks on the ground, branches, leaves, forests, fences, roads, bridges, houses, and friends are alike. Two red birds take us around several winter scenes as we ponder this notion. The book ends with the birds looking at each other and then flying off, leaving one feather each as we read: "Are we the same— just alike? Almost, *almost* . . . but not quite."

STORYTELLING TIPS: There's a nice, quiet lilt to this rhyming text. The images of snowflakes against a grayish blue sky background lend themselves to a hushed delivery.

Musical Activity

"Dance Like Snowflakes," traditional.

Sing to the tune of the traditional song "Frere Jacques." The melody can be found on the Internet as well as the following children's music recordings: *Corner Grocery Store* by Raffi (Troubadour, 1979) and *Wee Sing Around the World* by Pamela Beall and Susan Nipp (Price Stern Sloan, 1994). Ask everyone to stand and move slowly around the room with their hands waving overhead.

> Dance like snowflakes, dance like snowflakes,
> In the air, in the air, (*Begin to slowly lower hands.*)
> Whirling twirling snowflakes, whirling twirling snowflakes,
> (*Everyone slowly spins in a circle. Hands should be waving waist-high.*)
> Here and there, here and there. (*Lower hands and sit back down as if you are a snowflake landing on the ground.*)

Picture Book / Felt Story

***One-Dog Sleigh* by Mary Casanova. Illustrated by Ard Hoyt.**
Farrar, Straus and Giroux, 2013.

A young girl hitches her horse to a red sleigh and is ready to go on a fun winter ride. Her little dog joins her. They head into the woods where a squirrel on an overhead branch announces that it wants to ride in the sleigh, too. "Z nestled in." An owl wants to join them next. The girl replies, "Perhaps another day . . . It's a one-squirrel, one-dog sleigh." The owl ignores the girl, and "Owl SWOOPED in to stay." They are joined by bigger and bigger animals: Lynx, Deer, and Bear. The sleigh finally gets stuck in a snowdrift. Mouse leads the way to becoming unstuck. A bump sends all of the animals (except the dog) out of the sleigh and back into the woods. The girl guides the horse back home, "just me and my pal in a one-dog sleigh."

Picture Book

Red Sled by Lita Judge. Illustrated by the author. Atheneum, 2011.

A child carries a red sled through the snow with a "Scrinch scrunch scrunch scrunch scrinch scrunch." That evening, a bear runs off with the sled and has fun sliding in the winter night with other forest animals. They go "Alley-oop" and "fluoomp. . . . .ft" and, my favorite, "Gadung Gadung Gadung Gadung." The bear returns the sled to where it found it. The next morning, the child notices the bear's tracks in the snow and says, "Hmmm?" The next evening, the animals are at it again.

Closing Sound Effects Activity

"Winter Noises" by Rob Reid.

- -

Everyone stands. You may need to prompt those kids who live in warm areas and are not familiar with cold weather noises.

> Winter noises are so fun.
> Make them with me one by one.
> Tell me how it sounds when you shovel.
> (*Mime shoveling and make a scraping noise.*)
> Tell me how it sounds when a big person uses the snowblower.
> (*Mime pushing a snowblower and make a roaring noise.*)
> Tell me how it sounds when you go sledding down a hill.
> (*Sit down and rock side to side, making a swooshing noise.*)
> Tell me how it sounds when you throw a snowball at a tree.
> (*Stand and mime throwing and make a smack noise.*)
> Tell me how it sounds when you're outside playing in the snow.
> (*Everyone laughs and yells.*)

5 Fun Backup Picture Books

Brownie Groundhog and the Wintry Surprise by Susan Blackaby. Illustrated by Carmen Segovia. Sterling, 2013.

- -

Fox, Brownie Groundhog, and Bunny are sharing a quiet December picnic when Brownie announces she's going to "'sleep until spring.'" She warns Fox, "'And don't eat Bunny. She's company.'" Fox is sad with "no Brownie and nothing to do." He and Bunny break into Brownie's home. When Fox asks if he can borrow her scarf, Brownie sleepily replies, "'Beaky white, yam slippy, doony dizzer.'" Fox takes that as a yes. Fox keeps making noise until Brownie is finally fully awake. She goes outside and sees that Fox has made a wintry surprise by decorating a tree. They have a feast before Brownie returns to her bed.

Bunnies on Ice by Johanna Wright. Illustrated by the author.
Roaring Brook, 2013.

A bunny family enjoys ice-skating. One bunny child knows that when the conditions are right, it's important to eat a big breakfast, wear lots of clothes ("but not too many" as we barely see the bunny child in the big bundle of clothing), "have lots of fans" (the trees are full of watchful birds), and have an excellent "support team" (a.k.a. family).

Perfect Soup by Lisa Moser. Illustrated by Ben Mantle. Random House, 2010.

Murray the mouse is all set to make "the Perfect Soup" until he realizes that he's out of carrots. He puts on his mittens, hat, and scarf and heads out into the snowy weather. Murray runs past a snowman. A farmer promises Murray he'll give the mouse a carrot if he gets wood in return. Horse will help Murray haul the wood if Murray provides him with some jingle bells. Murray continues on his journey, all the time ignoring a beckoning snowman. After a long trek involving several other characters, Murray is helped by the snowman. Murray gives the snowman a surprise gift at the end of the book.

Pip and Posy: The Snowy Day by Axel Scheffler. Illustrated by the author.
Nosy Crow, 2012.

Posy the mouse and Pip the rabbit go outside to play in the snow. They make snow angels, catch snowflakes on their tongues, and go sledding. They start arguing, however, when Posy wants to build a snowmouse and Pip wants to make a snowrabbit. Posy throws a snowball at Pip, who then pushes Posy down in the snow. "Now Pip and Posy were both *very* cold and *very* sad." They apologize to each other and head inside to make clay mice and rabbits "and frogs and pigs and birds, and elephants and cows and giraffes!"

Utterly Otterly Night by Mary Casanova. Illustrated by Ard Hoyt. Simon & Schuster, 2011.

- -

Little Otter wants to leave his cozy winter den and play outside in the snow. Before he goes out, his mother warns him to watch out for danger. Little Otter and his family slide down a snowy hill until he "smells *trouble* on the breeze." Wolves are headed their way. Little Otter yells "Danger," but he's too far away for his family to hear. Little Otter leads the wolves on a chase until his family hears the warnings and all dive into the river. Once they are safe in their den, Little Otter falls asleep, dreaming of his "utterly otterly night."

ANIMALS AT NIGHT
STORIES AND ACTIVITIES ABOUT BEDTIME

★ Opening Picture Book: *Nighty-Night, Cooper* by Laura Numeroff and Lynn Munsinger

★ Picture Book: *I'm Not Sleepy!* by Jane Chapman

★ Sound Effects Activity: "While We Sleep" by Rob Reid

★ Picture Book: *Sleep like a Tiger* by Mary Logue and Pamela Zagarenski

★ Sound Effects Activity: "Animal Snores" by Rob Reid

★ Picture Book: *Boom! Boom! Boom!* by Jamie A. Swenson and David Walker

★ Movement Activity: "When Bears Wake Up" by Rob Reid

★ Closing Picture Book: *Let's Sing a Lullaby with the Brave Cowboy* by Jan Thomas

Opening Picture Book

Nighty-Night, Cooper by Laura Numeroff. Illustrated by Lynn Munsinger. Houghton Mifflin, 2013.

- -

Mama kangaroo sings bedtime songs to little Cooper. The first song is sung to the tune of "Rock-a-Bye Baby" and follows a pig sailing down the river past slumbering animals. "He'll see the cows / They're taking a snooze . . ." Cooper asks his mother to sing a song about mice next. She complies with this "Farmer in the Dell" inspired tune: "A mouse got into bed / A mouse got into bed / He tossed and turned, then fell asleep / And dreamt he found some bread." Mama eventually sings four more songs before *she* falls asleep.

> **STORYTELLING TIPS:** This is a fun picture book that combines straight narration with singing simple tunes. While singing, imagine yourself singing to one child. It might even help to have a stuffed toy kangaroo in your lap while playing the mama role.

Picture Book

I'm Not Sleepy! by Jane Chapman. Illustrated by the author. Good Books, 2012.

- -

Grandma Owl tries to put owlet Mo to bed. Mo wants to play. Grandma leaves but comes back when Mo reminds her that he hasn't had his snack. Grandma goes "Hop . . . Jump . . . Flutter . . . Flump! to the top of the tree" with a cookie. Mo keeps putting off bedtime.

> **STORYTELLING TIPS:** When you read the repetitive lines, "Hop . . . Jump . . . Flutter . . . Flump," have the children say the words with you. They can make two hopping motions with their hands and fingers for "Hop" and "Jump" and flap their arms like wings on "Flutter" and "Flump."

Mo decides that he'll "Hop . . . Jump . . . Flutter . . . Flump!" and put Grandma to bed. Mo does this over and over until, of course, he becomes very sleepy.

Sound Effects Activity

"While We Sleep" by Rob Reid.

- -

While we sleep, the owls do play,
And this is what those little owls say,
"Whoo-whoo! Whoo-whoo!"

While we sleep, the crickets do play,
And this is what those little crickets say,
"Chirp-chirp! Chirp-chirp!"

While we sleep, the frogs do play,
And this is what those little frogs say,
"Rib-it, croak! Rib-it, croak!"

While we sleep, the wolves do play,
And this is what those little wolves say,
"Howwwl! Howwwl!"

Picture Book

Sleep like a Tiger by Mary Logue. Illustrated by Pamela Zagarenski. Houghton Mifflin, 2012.

- -

A little girl did not want to go to sleep. "She told her mother, 'I'm not tired.' She told her father, 'I'm not sleepy.'" She put on her pajamas, washed her face, and climbed into bed. "'I'm still wide awake,' she announced." Her parents tell her that everything in the world goes to sleep, including dogs, cats, bats ("during the day they fold their wings, tuck in their heads, and sleep upside down"), whales, snails, and bears. The girl tells her parents that she knows the tiger sleeps, too. When her parents leave her bedroom, the girl imitates what she knows about the various animals and the way they sleep, ending with the tiger.

STORYTELLING TIPS: Bring the children close to you and inform them you'll be reading a very quiet book now. For the second half of the story, when the girl is reflecting on the animals her parents told her about, the audience members can stretch their bodies like the various animals and mime the actions. The dog curls up, the cat wriggles under the covers, the bats fold their wings, the whale circles around, the snail also curls up, the bear snuggles, and the tiger closes his eyes.

Sound Effects Activity

"Animal Snores" by Rob Reid.

Ask everyone what it sounds like when people snore. Kids will respond with a variety of snoring noises. Then show them what you think it would be like if a dog snored like a person. This activity first appeared in *LibrarySparks* magazine.

Dog snore: "Snore . . . woof, woof, woof . . . Snore . . . woof, woof, woof."

Have everyone join you with the following animal snores.

Cat snore: "Snore . . . meow, meow, meow . . . Snore . . . meow, meow, meow."
Cow snore: "Snore . . . moo, moo, moo . . . Snore . . . moo, moo, moo."
Chicken snore: "Snore . . . cluck, cluck, cluck . . . Snore . . . cluck, cluck, cluck."

Ask the kids for more animal suggestions.

Picture Book

Boom! Boom! Boom! by Jamie A. Swenson. Illustrated by David Walker. Farrar, Straus and Giroux, 2013.

- -

A little boy's dog seeks the safety of the boy's bed during a thunderstorm. "Two snuggled together to wait out the storm. Dog and I all comfy and warm." The noisy storm sends kitty, guinea pig, frog, parrot, snake—even sister—squished together in the boy's bed. When sister jumps in, the bed breaks, which sends all of the animals scurrying elsewhere. The storm ends, and the boy is alone in his broken bed with his book and his stuffed teddy bear Fred.

STORYTELLING TIPS: Before each animal arrives in the story, it is preceded by the storm noises: "FLASH! CRASH! BOOM! BOOM! BOOM!" Teach the kids in the audience to make this series of noises. Think of accompanying hand gestures for them to make. For example, they can "explode" their fingers with an upraised hand for "FLASH!" Do the same with the other hand for "CRASH!" And clap three times when yelling "BOOM! BOOM! BOOM!" If there are several parents in the room, they can yell the "FLASH! CRASH!" part and the kids can add the "BOOM! BOOM! BOOM!"

Movement Activity

"When Bears Wake Up" by Rob Reid.

- -

When bears wake up, they shake their head, (*Shake head.*)
They stretch their paws and crawl out of bed.
(*Stretch paws and stand. Then sit again.*)
When birds wake up, they shake their head, (*Shake head.*)
They flap their wings and fly out of bed.
(*Flap arms and fly in a circle. Sit again.*)
When snakes wake up, they shake their head, (*Shake head.*)

They stretch their tongues and slither out of bed.

(*Move tongue in and out and mime slithering. Sit again.*)

When kangaroos wake up, they shake their head, (*Shake head.*)

They pat their pouch and jump out of bed.

(*Pat tummy, jump up and down. Sit again.*)

When elephants wake up, they shake their head, (*Shake head.*)

They stretch their trunk and lumber out of bed.

(*Hold arm in front of nose, stand, and move side to side. Sit again.*)

When peacocks wake up, they shake their head, (*Shake head.*)

They flap their tails and run out of bed.

(*Stand, splay hands near bottom, and run in a circle. Sit again.*)

Closing Picture Book

Let's Sing a Lullaby with the Brave Cowboy by Jan Thomas. Illustrated by the author. Beach Lane, 2012.

- -

A guitar-toting cowboy starts to sing lullabies to two cows out on the prairie. After a few stanzas, the cowboy yells, "Eeeeek!" He sees a spider. The cows point out that "the spider" is really a flower. The cowboy resumes singing, but he stops again with another "Eeeeek!" This time, he thinks he sees a snake. "It's just a stick, Cowboy," says one cow. When the cowboy is worried he sees a "huge shaggy gray wolf," it turns out to be, indeed, a wolf. This time, the *cows* shout "Eeeeek!" The wolf convinces them that it *loves* lullabies and joins them, donning a nightcap.

STORYTELLING TIPS: Make up your own Western-style tune with a certain amount of twang while you simulate the cowboy's lullaby. "It's time for little cows to rest their heads / It's time for little cows to go to bed . . ." Know your audience and adjust the volume and "jump-factor" when you interrupt the song with an "Eeeeek!"

5 Fun Backup Picture Books

Chicks Run Wild by Sudipta Bardhan-Quallen. Illustrated by Ward Jenkins. Simon & Schuster, 2011.

- -

Mama chicken puts her five chicks to bed, but when she leaves their bedroom, "those chicks run wild!" They wiggle, jump, thump, and play until they hear tired Mama returning. When Mama peeks in the room, she sees the chicks in their beds "all catching zees." Mama doesn't truly believe her eyes, but kisses them each and leaves once again. As soon as she's gone, "those chicks run wild!" Mama finally chastises the chicks for not inviting her to join their fun.

Everyone Sleeps by Marcellus Hall. Illustrated by the author. Nancy Paulsen, 2013.

- -

A pet dog named Conrad roams through the house while his owners are sleeping. "Even the computer sleeps!" Conrad wonders if he's the only one not sleeping. We learn the various ways different animals sleep. "Horses sleep standing up. Snakes sleep lying down." We also learn about the sleeping traits of squirrels, rabbits, ducks, frogs, bears, bats, giraffes, fish and other "creatures of the deep," walruses, tigers, elephants, monkeys, foxes, otters, and sheep. Conrad starts counting those sleeping sheep, but still doesn't fall asleep himself. He finally notices someone else is awake—his young girl owner. They agree to try to fall asleep together.

It Is Night by Phyllis Rowand. Illustrated by Laura Dronzek. Greenwillow, 2014.

- -

The narrator asks where a bear would sleep. We turn the page and learn "in a cozy cave." We also learn about bedtime places for roosters, rabbits, ducks, cats, seals, dogs, elephants, mice, and monkeys. We even learn where dolls and railroad trains sleep: "If it is going somewhere, it goes there. And if it is not, it stands still on the tracks." We learn, in the end, that the animals and items named in the book are actually toys, and they sleep "in the bed of one small child . . . ALL OF THEM!"

No Sleep for the Sheep! by Karen Beaumont. Illustrated by Jackie Urbanovic. Harcourt, 2011.

A sleeping sheep is awoken by a loud "QUACK." The sheep implores the duck to be quiet, and both the duck and the sheep go to sleep. They are both awoken by a "BAAA." The sheep implores the goat to be quiet. The goat falls asleep with the sheep and the duck. This pattern continues with a pig going "OINK," a cow going "MOO," and a horse going "NEIGHHHHHH." In the morning, almost all are awoken by the rooster's "COCK-A-DOODLE-DOO!" "But the sheep slept right on through."

Piggies in Pajamas by Michelle Meadows. Illustrated by Ard Hoyt. Simon & Schuster, 2013.

While Mama pig is on the phone, the piggy children make a lot of noise instead of sleeping. They go "THUMP, THUMP, OINK, OINK," and "TOOT, TOOT, OINK, OINK," and "BOOM, BOOM, OINK, OINK." Each time they hear a "STOMP, STOMP, STOMP, STOMP," they run back to bed waiting to see if Mama is coming. The little piggies finally settle down with a "SNUGGLE, SNUGGLE, GOOD NIGHT."

INDEX

Titles of fingerplays, songs, and poems are shown in quotes.
Titles of books and CDs are shown in italic.